Tipping recommendations

Tipping is, of course, a matter of personal appreciation. But there are a few musts: for example, if you come back to your hotel after 11 p.m. and you have to ring the bell, you should give something to the doorman. Cloakroom attendants generally expect a tip. And when you make a phone call, leave the odd bit of loose change for that service, too. A small gift will be appreciated by tour guides. The chart below makes some suggestions as to how much to leave.

HOTEL	
Service charge, bill	10% included
Porter, per bag	20 złotys
Bellboy, errand	10 złotys
Chambermaid	optional
Doorman, hails cab	10 złotys
RESTAURANT	
Service charge, bill	10% included
Waiter	round off upwards
Cloakroom attendant	charges posted, or 5 złotys
Lavatory attendant	5 złotys
Taxi driver	10%
Men's barber	5–10%
Women's hairdresser	10%
Tour guide	small gift (optional)

BERLITZ PHRASE BOOKS

World's bestselling phrase books feature not only expressions and vocabulary you'll need, but also travel tips, useful facts and pronunciation throughout. The handiest and most readable conversation aid available.

Arabic	French	Polish
Chinese	German	Portuguese
Danish	Greek	Russian
Dutch	Hebrew	Serbo-Croatian
European	Hungarian	Spanish
(14 languages)	Italian	Lat.-Am. Spanish
European	Japanese	Swahili
Menu Reader	Korean	Swedish
Finnish	Norwegian	Turkish

BERLITZ CASSETTEPAKS

The above-mentioned titles are also available combined with a cassette to help you improve your accent. A helpful miniscript is included containing the complete text of the dual language hi-fi recording.

BERLITZ®

POLISH
FOR TRAVELLERS

By the staff of Berlitz Guides

Preface

You are about to visit Poland. Our aim has been to produce a practical phrase book to help you on your trip.

Polish for Travellers provides:

* all the phrases and supplementary vocabulary you will need on your trip

* a wide variety of tourist and travel facts, tips and useful information

* a complete phonetic transcription, showing you the pronunciation of all the words and phrases listed

* special sections showing the replies your listener might give to you. Just hand him the book and let him point to the appropriate phrase. This is especially practical in certain difficult situations (doctor, car mechanic, etc.). It makes direct, quick and sure communication possible

* a logical system of presentation so that you can find the right phrase for the immediate situation

* quick reference through colour coding. The major features of the contents are on the back cover; a complete index is given inside.

These are just a few of the practical advantages. In addition, the book will prove a valuable introduction to life in Poland.

There is a comprehensive section on Eating Out, giving translations and explanations for practically anything one would find on a menu in Poland; there is a complete Shopping Guide that will enable you to obtain virtually anything you want. Trouble with the car? Turn to the mechanic's manual with its dual-language instructions. Feeling ill? Our medical section provides the most rapid communication possible between you and the doctor.

To make the most of *Polish for Travellers,* we suggest that you start with the "Guide to Pronunciation". Then go on to "Some Basic Expressions". This not only gives you a minimum vocabulary; it helps you to pronounce the language.

We are particularly grateful to Dr. James Pankhurst for his help in the preparation of this book, and also to Dr. T.J.A. Bennett for his help in creating the phonetic transcription. Additionally, we wish to thank Ars Polona for their assistance.

We shall be very pleased to receive any comments, criticisms and suggestions that you think may help us in preparing future editions.

Thank you. Have a good trip.

Guide to pronunciation

This and the following chapter are intended to make you familiar with the phonetic transcription we devised and to help you get used to the sounds of Polish.

As a minimum vocabulary for your trip, we have selected a number of basic words and phrases under the title "Some Basic Expressions" (pages 11–16).

An outline of the spelling and sounds of Polish

You will find the pronunciation of the Polish letters and sounds explained below, as well as the symbols we're using for them in the transcriptions. Note that Polish has some diacritical letters —letters with accent marks—which we do not know in English.

The imitated pronunciation should be read as if it were English except for any special rules set out below. Of course, the sounds of any two languages are never exactly the same; but if you follow carefully the indications supplied here, you will have no difficulty in reading our transcriptions in such a way as to make yourself understood.

Letters shown in bold print should be read with more stress (louder) than the others.

Consonants

Letter	Approximate pronunciation	Symbol	Example	
b, f, k, l, m, p, z	are pronounced as in English			
cz	as the English **ch** in **ch**urch	ch	**czy**	chi

dż	as the English j in jam	j	dżem	jehm
g	as in English girl	g	guma	gumah
j	as the English y in yet	y	jak	yahk
ł	as the English w in win	w	ładny	wahdni
n	as in English but put your tongue against the front teeth and not the teeth ridge	n	na	nah
s	as the English s in sit	s	sam	sahm
sz	as the English sh in shine	sh	szal	shahl
t, d	as in English but put your tongue against the front teeth and not against the teeth ridge	t d	tak dom	tahk dom
w	as the English v in van	v	woda	vodah
ż or rz	as the English s in pleasure	zh	żelazo rzeka	zhehlahzo zhehkah

Sounds distinctly different

An often recurring phenomenon in the Slavic languages is "softening", or the "softened" pronunciation of consonants. Examples of this in Polish are ć, dź, ń, ś and ź. A similar effect can be produced by pronouncing y as in yet—but very, very short—after the consonant.

c	like the English sequence ts in tsetse pronounced quickly	ts	co	tso
ć	pronounced like the Polish c but in a much softer way	tsh	ciało	tshahwo
dz	like the English sequence ds in beds pronounced quickly	dz	dzwonek	dzvonehk
dź or dzi	pronounced like the Polish dz but in a much softer way	dzh	dział	dzhahw

PRONUNCIATION

h or ch	similar to English h but with much more friction	h	**herbata** **chudy**	hehr**bah**tah **hoo**di
ń or ni	pronounced like the English n with considerable softening	ñ	**nie**	ñeh
r	like the Scottish r (vibration of the tongue); note that it is also pronounced at the end of words	r	**rak**	rahk
ś or si	pronounced like the English s but in a much softer way. Note that it is one sound, not two; i.e., the transcription **ktosy** should never be pronounced as **ktos-y**	sy	**się** **ktoś**	syeh ktosy
ź or zi	pronounced like the English z but in a much softer way	zy	**zielony**	zyeh**lo**ni

Notice that voiced sounds become completely devoiced at the end of a word or in the context of other voiceless sounds, i.e., they are pronounced like their voiceless counterparts (e.g., **b** of chle**b** is pronounced like **p**; **w** of ró**w** is pronounced like **f**; **rz** and **z** in p**rz**e**z** like **sz** and **s**, etc.).

Vowels

a	as English u in cult	ah	**tak**	tahk
e	like English e of ten	eh	**lek**	lehk
i	as English ee in feet	ee	**ile**	**ee**leh
y	as English i in fit	i	**ty**	ti
o	as English o in cot	o	**kot**	kot
u or ó	as the sound between the English u of put and oo of boots	oo	**drut**	droot

| ą | is pronounced **on** before a consonant; when it's the final letter, it is pronounced as the **an** in the French—like pronunciation of the word fiancé | on awng | **prąd** **są** | pront sawng |
| ę | is pronounced **en** before a consonant or like **e** in bed when it is the final letter | ehn eh | **pęd** **tę** | pehnt teh |

Some diphthongs

| ej | as English **a** in take | ay | **dobrej** | dobray |
| aj | as English **i** in like | igh | **daj** | digh |

The stress falls in Polish on the next to the last syllable, e.g. **głodny** (**gwod**ni), **drogeria** (drogeh**ryah**).

Some basic expressions

Yes.	**Tak**.	tahk
No.	**Nie.**	ñeh
Please.	**Proszę.**	prosheh
Thank you.	**Dziękuję.**	dzhehnkooyeh
Thank you very much.	**Dziękuję bardzo.**	dzhehnkooyeh bahrdzo
That's all right.	**Proszę bardzo.**	prosheh bahrdzo

Greetings

Good morning.	**Dzień dobry.**	dzhehñ dobri
Good afternoon.	**Dzień dobry.**	dzhehñ dobri
Good evening.	**Dobry wieczór.**	dobri vyehchoor
Good night.	**Dobranoc.**	dobrahnots
Good-bye.	**Do widzenia.**	do veedzehñah
See you later.	**Do zobaczenia.**	do zobahchehñah
This is Mr. ...	**To jest pan...**	to yehst pahn
This is Mrs. ...	**To jest pani...**	to yehst pahñee
This is Miss...	**To jest pani...**	to yehst pahñee
I'm very pleased to meet you.	**Miło mi pana/ panią poznać.**	meewo mee pahna/ pahñawng poznahtsh
How are you?	**Jak się pan/pani miewa?**	yahk syeh pahn/pahñee myehvah

There's often a difference in grammatical form depending upon whether the person speaking is a man or a woman. We've used masculine forms throughout in this book except in cases where the feminine seemed more appropriate.

Very well, thank you.	**Bardzo dobrze, dziękuję.**	**bah**rdzo **do**bzheh dzhehn**koo**yeh
And you?	**A pan/pani?**	ah pahn/**pah**ñee
Fine.	**Dobrze.**	**do**bzheh
Excuse me.	**Przepraszam.**	psheh**prah**shahm

Questions

Where?	**Gdzie?**	gdzheh
Where is...?	**Gdzie jest...?**	gdzheh yehst
Where are...?	**Gdzie są...?**	gdzheh sawng
When?	**Kiedy?**	**kyeh**di
What?	**Co?**	tso
How?	**Jak?**	yahk
How much?	**Ile?**	**ee**leh
How many?	**Ile?**	**ee**leh
Who?	**Kto?**	kto
Why?	**Dlaczego?**	dlah**cheh**go
Which?	**Który?**	**ktoo**ri
What do you call this?	**Jak się to nazywa?**	yahk syeh to nah**zi**vah
What do you call that?	**Jak się tamto nazywa?**	yahk syeh **tahm**to nah**zi**vah
What does this mean?	**Co to znaczy?**	tso to **znah**chi
What does that mean?	**Co tamto znaczy?**	tso **tahm**to **znah**chi

Do you speak...?

Do you speak English?	**Czy pan/pani mówi po angielsku?**	chi pahn/**pah**ñee **moo**vee po ahn**gyehl**skoo
Do you speak German?	**Czy pan/pani mówi po niemiecku?**	chi pahn/**pah**ñee **moo**vee po nyeh**myeh**tskoo
Do you speak French?	**Czy pan/pani mówi po francusku?**	chi pahn/**pah**ñee **moo**vee po frahn**tsoo**skoo

Do you speak Spanish?	Czy pan/pani mówi po hiszpańsku?	chi pahn/pahñee moovee po heeshpahñskoo
Do you speak Italian?	Czy pan/pani mówi po włosku?	chi pahn/pahñee moovee po vwoskoo
Could you speak more slowly, please?	Proszę mówić trochę wolniej.	prosheh mooveetsh troheh volñay
Please point to the phrase in the book.	Proszę wskazać odpowiednie zdanie w moich rozmówkach.	prosheh fskahzahtsh otpovyehdñeh zdahñeh vmoeeh rozmoofkahh
Just a minute. I'll see if I can find it in this book.	Chwileczkę. Zobaczę czy to jest w moich rozmówkach.	hfeelehchkeh. zobahcheh chi to yehst vmoee⁀ rozmoofkahh
I understand.	Rozumiem.	rozoomyehm
I don't understand.	Nie rozumiem.	ñeh rozoomyehm

Can...?

Can I have...?	Czy mogę dostać...?	chi mogeh dostahtsh
Can we have...?	Czy możemy dostać...?	chi mozhehmy dostahtsh
Can you show me...?	Czy może mi pan/pani pokazać...?	chi mozheh mee pahn/pahñee pokahzahtsh
Can you tell me...?	Czy może mi pan/pani powiedzieć...?	chi mozheh mee pahn/pahñee povyehdzhehtsh
Can you help me, please?	Czy może mi pan/pani pomóc?	chi mozheh mee pahn/pahñee pomoots

Wanting

I'd like...	Chciałbym...	htshahwbim
We'd like...	Chcielibyśmy...	htshehleebisymi
Please give me...	Proszę mi dać...	prosheh mee dahtsh
Give it to me, please.	Proszę mi to dać.	prosheh mee to dahtsh

Please bring me...	**Proszę przynieść mi...**	**pro**sheh pshiñehsytsh mee
Bring it to me, please.	**Proszę mi to przynieść.**	**pro**sheh mee to pshiñehsytsh
I'm hungry.	**Jestem głodny.**	**yeh**stehm gwodni
I'm thirsty.	**Chce mi się pić.**	htseh mee syeh peetsh
I'm tired.	**Jestem zmęczony.**	**yeh**stehm zmehnchoni
I'm lost.	**Zgubiłem się.**	zgoobee**weh**m syeh
It's important.	**To ważne.**	to **vah**zhneh
It's urgent.	**To pilne.**	to **peel**neh
Hurry up!	**Niech się pan/ pani pospieszy!**	ñehh syeh pahn/**pah**ñee pos**pyeh**shi

It is/There is...

It is/It's...	**To jest...**	to yehst
Is it...?	**Czy to jest...?**	chi to yehst
It isn't...	**To nie jest...**	to ñeh yehst
There is/There are...	**Jest/Są...**	yehst/sawng
Is there/Are there...?	**Czy jest/Czy są...?**	chi yehst/chi sawng
There isn't/There aren't...	**Nie ma...**	ñeh mah
There isn't any/ There aren't any.	**Nie ma.**	ñeh mah

A few common words

big/small	**duży/mały**	**doo**zhi/**mah**wi
quick/slow	**szybki/wolny**	**ship**kee/**vol**ni
early/late	**wczesny/późny**	**fcheh**sni/**poo**zyni
cheap/expensive	**tani/drogi**	**tah**ñee/**dro**gee
near/far	**bliski/daleki**	**blees**kee/**dah**lehkee
hot/cold	**gorący/zimny**	go**ront**si/**zyeem**ni

full/empty	pełny/pusty	pehwni/poosti
easy/difficult	łatwy/trudny	wahtfi/troodni
heavy/light	ciężki/lekki	tshehnshkee/lehkkee
open/shut	otwarty/ zamknięty	otfahrti/zahmkñehnti
right/wrong	słuszny/ niesłuszny	swooshni/ñehswooshni
old/new	stary/nowy	stahri/novi
old/young	stary/młody	stahri/mwodi
beautiful/ugly	piękny/brzydki	pyehnkni/bzhitkee
good/bad	dobry/zły	dobri/zwi
better/worse	lepiej/gorzej	lehpyay/gozhay

A few prepositions and some more useful words

at	przy	pshi
on	na	nah
in	w	v
to	do	do
from	z	z
inside	wewnątrz	vehvnontsh
outside	na zewnątrz	nah zehvnontsh
up	do góry	do goori
down	na dół	nah doow
before	przed	psheht
after	po	po
with	z	z
without	bez	behs
through	przez	pshehs
towards	w kierunku	fkyehroonkoo
until	aż do	ahzh do
during	podczas	potchahs

16

and	**i**	ee
or	**lub**	loop
not	**nie**	ñeh
nothing	**nic**	ñeets
none	**żaden**	zhahdehn
very	**bardzo**	bahrdzo
also	**też/także**	tehsh/tahgzheh
soon	**wkrótce**	fkroottseh
perhaps	**może**	mozheh
here	**tutaj**	tootigh
there	**tam**	tahm
now	**teraz**	tehrahs
then	**potem**	potehm

A very basic grammar

Polish is a member of the Slavonic family of languages, along with Czech, Serbo-Croatian, Russian and a number of others. What is most striking about it is a very formidable and functionally important case system. This makes Polish seem more like Latin or Old English than present-day English or French. But it is not necessary to master the case system in order to use this phrase book, and rather than confuse you with a lot of facts that you won't be able to assimilate, this section aims at giving you some interesting insight into how the language works and what its general structure is like.

The spelling of Polish looks extremely forbidding, although it is what is generally described as a phonetic language. This is partly because a number of sounds are represented by a cluster of two separate letters (like "sh" and "ch" in English). But in any case, consonant sounds really do mass together in this language and you will find that Poles delight in giving foreigners some real tongue-twisters to pronounce.

If you look carefully at Polish words, it won't be long before you come to realise that many of them are related to English words; usually though, the relationship goes far back into history and isn't often close enough to enable you to guess the meaning of words. While the relationship between **mleko** and its English translation "milk" is fairly apparent, it requires some imagination to recognise the relationship between **chleb** (bread) and the English word "loaf". Nevertheless, the relationship is there.

Nouns
Nouns change their case forms according to their function in the sentence, according to the preposition they follow, and even according to whether the verb of the sentence is negated or not.

GRAMMAR

The plural of nouns is not formed in just one way, as is the case with English, but also has a whole set of different forms. The main case forms that will concern you in this book are the nominative singular (or dictionary form) of the word and the accusative singular direct object. The latter is sometimes the same as the nominative but very often ends in ę. Adjectives usually precede their nouns and agree with them in number, gender and case.

Incidentally, there are no definite or indefinite articles in Polish, so in the text you will find no translation of "a" or "the". On the other hand, when some Poles speak to you in English, you may notice a tendency not to use articles.

Verbs

Verbs normally appear in Polish without any pronoun because the endings of the verb indicate the subject sufficiently. There are at least six different endings for each tense, and there are three main tenses. In the past tense there are even different forms according to whether the subject of the verb is masculine, feminine or neuter gender! This sometimes occurs in our book; where needed, feminine forms of the past tense are given as an alternative.

But for practical purposes you can make do with just three forms of the present:

1. The form used with **pan** ("you" said to a man) and **pani** ("you" said to a woman), which usually ends in **e**;

2. The form used when the subject is "we", known as the first person plural, usually ending in **imy** or **emy**;

3. The form used with **państwo** (the plural form of **pan** and **pani**), or when the subject is "they". This form usually ends in **ą**.

The first person singular form (used with "I") is virtually identical to the third person singular (the form used with **pan**, and **pani**), usually ending in **ę**. Here, then, is the conjugation in the present tense of the verb **studiować** (to study):

I study	(ja) studiuję	we study	(my) studiujemy
you study	pan/pani studiuje	you study (pl.)	państwo studiują
he studies	(on) studiuje	they study (m.)	(oni) studiują
she studies	(ona) studiuje	they study (f.)	(one) studiują

Another translation of "you study" is **(ty) studiujesz.** There has to be some degree of intimacy or comradeship for this form to be acceptable. **Ty** (you) will almost always be omitted.

Of the irregular verbs, the three most useful for you to be familiar with are **być** (to be), **mieć** (to have) and **iść** (to go). Given below are the conjugations of these verbs in the present tense:

		to be	to have	to go
I	(ja)	jestem	mam	idę
you	pan/pani	jest	ma	idzie
he/she	(on/ona)	jest	ma	idzie
we	(my)	jesteśmy	mamy	idziemy
you (pl.)	państwo	są	mają	idą
they	(oni/one)	są	mają	idą

Forms of address

A man is addressed as **pan**, which can mean "man", "Mr." or "sir"; a woman (married or single) is addressed as **pani**. As indicated above, instead of a pronoun corresponding to the English "you", **pan** or **pani** is used. It is more polite to refer to someone indirectly without "you", even in English. Thus we sometimes hear: "What does madam want?" In Polish, if we want to say "you are going", we say **pan idzie**.

You will notice that native speakers sprinkle their conversation with **proszę pana** (literally, "please, sir") and **proszę pani** ("please, madam"). This is strictly a polite gap filler, but will always go well at the beginning of any utterance. **Proszę** (please) can be used to ask for anything, e.g., **proszę kawę** means "coffee, please", or – if you like – "I want some coffee", or "May I have some coffee?" If there is more than one of you, say it in the plural: **prosimy**.

GRAMMAR

Asking questions and saying "no"

Polish is an easy language to ask questions in: they are exactly like statements, except that they are said with a rising intonation. Thus "John is going" will be a question or a statement according to your intonation. Optionally, a question can begin with the question word **czy**, which has no meaning except to indicate the beginning of a question. We have used this word regularly in this book, just in case your intonation falters.

There is just one word in Polish for "no" and "not". It is **nie**, and to make a sentence negative you just put **nie** before the verb. Thus to say: "No, I don't speak Polish", you just say: **"Nie, nie mówię po polsku."** One very curious thing about negation in Polish is that if you ask a question such as "Is there any bread?" (**Czy jest chleb?**), the answer you might well get would be **Nie ma chleba**. What has happened here with the verb **jest** (a form of the verb "to be" in Polish) is that it has completely changed and become the verb "have" (**ma**); moreover, as has already been mentioned, negation involves a case change in the noun. These facts are put in here to give you some idea of the complexity of structure in Polish, not because you should try to master them. Unless you take up Polish seriously, you won't be able to handle this kind of subtlety, but you will be understood just the same.

Word order

Nouns and verbs do not follow a regular pattern of word order as is the case in English. The relationship between them is shown largely by case endings. Thus it is possible for the Polish version of the phrase "John gave Mary the radio" to appear in a large number of different order patterns. The subject will not necessarily appear before the verb, as it does in English, but will definitely be in a particular case. There will be other clues, too. For example, the form of the verb will tell us whether John, Mary or the radio is the subject because the verb in the past tense will have a special ending indicating the gender of the subject noun.

Although word order appears pretty free, there are some factors that do determine it in Polish. These are largely factors of emphasis: words that are to be given prominence tend to appear in sentence initial or sentence final position. One kind of mistake then that you won't be making very much in Polish is mistakes in word order.

Attitudes to correctness

Your attempts to communicate in Polish are sure to result in enthusiasm on the part of the Poles you are speaking to, and they will be very tolerant of your errors. Within the country, however, there are very strongly developed attitudes towards correctness. Standard Polish is recognised and is in fact much more widespread than is standard English in America or Britain. This has a historical explanation: during the years of partition in the last century, the language itself was largely suppressed by the occupying powers. This resulted in very determined attempts by Poles to keep their language alive and for some time it was explicitly taught just like a second language. This has had the effect of making the standard form much more widespread than it would have been and has led to the eradication of many regional differences.

Arrival

You've arrived. Whether you've come by ship, train or plane, you'll have to go through passport and customs formalities. (For car/border control, see page 145.)

There's certain to be somebody around who speaks English. That's why we're making this a brief section. What you really want is to be off to your hotel in the shortest possible time. Here are the stages for a speedy departure.

Passport Control

Give your passport and visa to the officer at the passport check. These'll be stamped and returned to you, but just in case there are any questions:

I'll be staying in Poland…	**Będę w Polsce…**	behndeh fpolstseh
a few days	**kilka dni**	keelkah dñee
a week	**tydzień**	tidzhehñ
two weeks	**dwa tygodnie**	dvah tigodñeh
a month	**miesiąc**	myehsyonts
I don't know yet.	**Jeszcze nie wiem.**	yehshcheh ñeh vyehm
I'm here on holidays.	**Jestem tu na wakacjach.**	yehstehm too nah vahkahtsyahh
I'm here on business.	**Jestem tu służbowo.**	yehstehm too swoozhbovo
I'm just passing through.	**Jestem przejazdem.**	yehstehm pshehyahzdehm

If things become difficult:

I'm sorry, I don't understand. Is there anyone here who speaks English?	**Przepraszam, nie rozumiem. Czy mówi tu ktoś po angielsku?**	pshehprahsham ñeh rozoomyehm. chi moovee too ktosy po ahngehlskoo

Customs

The chart below shows you what you can bring in duty free*.

Cigarettes	Cigars	Tobacco (grams)	Liquor (spirits)	Wine
250 or	50 or	250	1 and	1

Currency restrictions: No złotys may be imported or exported. Import and export (up to the amount brought in) of foreign currencies is unlimited. A currency declaration form must be completed on arrival and presented again on departure. Western visitors are required to purchase (through Orbis, the national travel organization) currency-exchange vouchers before coming to Poland.

I have nothing to declare.	**Nie mam nic do zadeklarowania.**	ñeh mahm ñeets do zahdehklahrovahñah
I have...	**Mam...**	mahm
a carton of cigarettes	**karton papierosów**	kahrton pahpyehrosoof
a bottle of whisky	**butelkę whisky**	bootehlkeh wiskee
a bottle of wine	**butelkę wina**	bootehlkeh veenah
Must I pay on this?	**Czy za to płacę cło?**	chi zah to pwahtseh tswo
How much?	**Ile?**	eeleh
It's for my personal use.	**To jest do użytku osobistego.**	to yehst do oozhitkoo osobistehgo
It's not new.	**To nie jest nowe.**	to ñeh yehst noveh

ARRIVAL

* All allowances subject to change without notice.

Possible answers

Od tego pan/pani musi zapłacić cło.	You'll have to pay duty on this.
Czy ma pan/pani więcej bagażu?	Have you any more luggage?
Proszę otworzyć tę torbę.	Open this bag, please.

Baggage—Porters

Where no porters are available, you'll find luggage trolleys for the use of passengers.

Porter!	Bagażowy!	bahgahzhovı
Can you help me with my luggage?	Proszę pomóc mi nieść te walizki.	prosheh pomoots mee ñehsytsh teh vahleeskee
That's mine.	To moje.	to moyeh
That's my...	To...	to
bag/luggage/ suitcase	moja torba/mój bagaż/moja walizka	moyah torbah/mooy bahgahsh/moyah vahleeskah
That... one.	Tę...	teh
big/small brown/black	dużą/małą brązową/czarną	doozhawng/mahwawng bronzovawng/chahrnawng
There's one missing.	Jednej brakuje.	yehdnay brahkooyeh
Take these bags to the taxi/bus.	Proszę zanieść te torby do taksówki/ autobusu.	prosheh zahñehsytsh teh torbi do tahksoofkee/ ahwtoboosoo
Get me a taxi, please.	Proszę spro- wadzić taksówkę.	prosheh sprovahdzheetsh tahksoofkeh
Where's the bus for the air terminal?	Gdzie jest autobus Lotu?	gdzheh yehst ahwtoboos lotoo
How much is that?	Ile płacę?	eeleh pwahtseh

Changing money

You'll find a currency-exchange counter at the international airport. If it's closed, don't worry. You'll be able to change money at your hotel.

Full details about money and exchange are given on pages 134–136.

Can you cash a traveller's cheque (check)?	Czy może mi pan/ pani wymienić czek podróżny?	chi mozheh mee pahn/ pahñee vimyehñeetsh chehk podroozhni
I want to change some...	Chcę wymienić...	htseh vimyehñeetsh
traveller's cheques	czeki podróżne	chehkee podroozhneh
dollars	dolary	dolahri
pounds	funty	foonti
Where's the nearest currency exchange?	Gdzie mogę najbliżej wymienić pieniądze?	gdzheh mogeh nighbleezhay vimyehñeetsh pyehñondzeh
What's the exchange rate?	Jaki jest kurs wymiany?	yahkee yehst koors vimyahni

Directions

How do I get to...?	Jak się dostać do...?	yahk syeh dostahtsh do
Is there a bus to the centre of town?	Czy jest autobus do centrum?	chi yehst ahwtoboos do tsehntroom
Where can I get a taxi?	Gdzie mogę dostać taksówkę?	gdzheh mogeh dostahtsh tahksoofkeh
Where can I rent a car?	Gdzie mogę wynająć samochód?	gdzheh mogeh vinighontsh sahmohoot

Hotel reservations

Many terminals have a tourist information office. You're sure to find somebody there who speaks English. The information office will be able to direct you to hotels.

FOR NUMBERS, see page 175

Car rental

Again, it's best to make arrangements in advance whenever possible. There's a car rental desk at the international airport and major hotels. You rent cars by the day, and there's a small mileage charge (some credit cards are accepted). It's highly likely that someone there'll speak English. But if nobody does, try one of the following…

Where can I rent a car?	Gdzie mogę wynająć samochód?	gdzheh mogeh vinighyońtsh sahmohoot
I'd like…	Chciałbym wynająć…	htshahwbim vinighyontsh
a car	samochód	sahmohoot
a small car	mały samochód	mahwi sahmohoot
a large car	duży samochód	doozhi sahmohoot
I'd like it for…	Chcę go na…	htseh go nah
a day/four days	dzień/cztery dni	dzhehń/chtehri dñee
a week/two weeks	tydzień/dwa tygodnie	tidzhehń/dvah tigodñeh
What's the charge per day?	Ile się płaci za dzień?	eeleh syeh pwahtshee zah dzhehń
What's the charge per week?	Ile się płaci za tydzień?	eeleh syeh pwahtshee zah tidzhehń
I've a credit card.	Mam kartę kredytową.	mahm kahrteh krehditovawng
Here's my driving licence.	To jest moje prawo jazdy.	to yehst moyeh prahvo yahzdi

Note: In Poland an international licence is required.

FOR SIGHTSEEING, see page 75

Taxi

You can get a taxi at a taxi-stand, hail one in the street or order one by telephone. All taxis have meters. Charges are higher at night and beyond the city limits.

Where can I get a taxi?	Gdzie są taksówki?	gdzheh sawng tahksoofkee
Get me a taxi, please.	Proszę sprowadzić mi taksówkę.	prosheh sprovahdzheetsh mee tahksoofkeh
What's the fare to…?	Ile kosztuje przejazd do…?	EEleh koshtooyeh psheh-yahst do
How far is it to…?	Jak daleko jest do…?	yahk dahlehko yehst do
Take me to…	Proszę mnie zawieźć…	prosheh mñeh zahvyehsytsh
this address	na ten adres	nah tehn ahdrehs
the town centre	do centrum	do tsehntroom
the… hotel	do hotelu…	do hotehloo
Turn left/right at the next corner.	Proszę skręcić w lewo/prawo na następnym rogu.	prosheh skrehntsheetsh vlehvo/prahvo nah nahstehmpnim rogoo
Go straight ahead.	Prosto.	prosto
Stop here, please.	Proszę się zatrzymać.	prosheh syeh zahchshi-mahtsh
I'm in a hurry.	Spieszy mi się.	spyehshi mee syeh
There's no hurry	Nie spieszy mi się.	ñeh spyehshi mee syeh
Could you drive more slowly?	Proszę jechać wolniej.	prosheh yehhahtsh volñay
Would you please wait for me?	Czy może pan/pani na mnie poczekać?	chi mozheh pahn/pahñee nah mñeh pochehkahtsh

ARRIVAL

FOR TIPPING, see page 1

Hotel—Other accommodation

Early reservation (and confirmation) is essential in cities and tourist centres throughout the year. Unless you're camping you'll probably have booked your accommodation before setting out for Poland, but if you haven't, go to the nearest Orbis office. This is the national tourist office, and they handle all bookings.

Hotels (and restaurants) are classified as Lux (luxury), S (special), first or second class. Service and appointments in the first two categories are excellent; many first-class hotels have rooms with bath and toilet. If the hotels are all booked or if you specially request it, Orbis may arrange for you to stay with a private family. In tourist centres, Orbis also runs boarding houses *(pensjonaty*—pehnsyo**nah**ti) which are good value for money. At seaside resorts or in the mountains you'll see houses with a card saying *pokój* (**po**kooy—room to let). This may be just what you need.

In holiday centres you'll notice many hotel-type buildings which in fact aren't open to the public. They belong to enterprises or institutions and offer first-class holiday accommodation to employees.

Many new hotels are planned to meet the growth of tourism, but if you don't like booking in advance and want to roam the country at leisure, why not try camping (see page 90)? If you're going to stay in hotels, this section will be helpful. In the big hotels you'll usually find members of staff who speak English but there are occasions when you don't.

In the next few pages we consider your requirements—step by step—from arrival to departure. You need not read through the whole lot; just turn to the situation that applies.

HOTEL

Checking in—Reception

My name is...	Moje nazwisko...	moyeh nahzveesko
I've a reservation.	Mam rezerwację.	mahm rehzehrvahtsyeh
We've reserved two rooms, a single and a double.	Zarezerwowałem dwa pokoje, pojedyńczy i podwójny.	zahrehzehrvovahwehm dvah pokoyeh poyehdiñchi ee podvooyni
I booked last month. Here's the confirmation.	Rezerwowałem w zeszłym mie-siącu. Oto kwit.	rehzehrvovahwehm vzeshwim myehsyontsoo. oto kfeet
I'd like...	Proszę...	proshe
single room	pojedyńczy pokój	poyehdiñchi pokooy
double room	podwójny pokój	podvooyni pokooy
two single rooms	dwa pojedyńcze pokoje	dvah poyendiñcheh pokoye
room with a bath	pokój z łazienką	pokooy zwahzyehnkawng
room with a shower	pokój z prysznicem	pokooy sprishñeetsehm
room with a balcony	pokój z balkonem	pokooy zbahlkonehm
room with a view	pokój z widokiem	pokooy zveedokehm
suite	apartament	ahpahrtahmehnt
We'd like a room...	Chcemy pokój...	htsehmi pokooy
in the front/at the back	od frontu/od tyłu	ot frontoo/ot tiwoo
facing the sea	z widokiem na morze	zveedokehm nah mozheh
It must be quiet.	Musi być cichy.	moosyee bitsh tsheehi
Is there...?	Czy jest...?	chi yehst
radio in the room	radio w pokoju	rahdyo fpokoyoo
television in the room	telewizor w pokoju	tehlehveezor fpokoyoo
hot water	ciepła woda	tshehpwah vodah
running water	bieżąca woda	byehzhontsah vodah
private toilet	osobna toaleta	osobnah twahlehta
Is there a laundry service?	Czy można oddać bieliznę do prania w hotelu?	chi mozhnah oddatsh byehleezneh do prahñah fhotehloo

HOTEL

How much?

What's the price...?	Ile kosztuje...?	eeleh koshtooyeh
per week	za tydzień	zah tidzhehñ
per night	za noc	zah nots
excluding meals	bez posiłków	behs posyeewkoof
for full board (American plan)	z pełnym utrzymaniem	spehwnim oochshimahñehm
Does that include...?	Czy to obejmuje...?	chi to obaymooyeh
breakfast	śniadanie	syñahdahñeh
meals	posiłki	posyeewkee
service	obsługę	opswoogeh
Is there any reduction for children?	Czy jest zniżka dla dzieci?	chi yehst zñeeshkah dlah dzhehtshee
Do you charge for the baby?	Czy płaci się za niemowlę?	chi pwahtshee syeh zah ñehmovleh
That's too expensive.	To za drogo.	to zah drogo
Haven't you anything cheaper?	Czy nie ma czegoś tańszego?	chi ñeh mah chehgosy tahñshehgo

How long?

We'll be staying...	Będziemy...	behñdzhehmi
overnight only	tylko jedną dobę	tilko yehdnawng dobeh
a few days	kilka dni	keelkah dñee
a week (at least)	tydzień (co najmniej)	tidzhehñ (tsonighmñay)
I don't know yet.	Nie wiem jeszcze.	ñeh vyehm yehshcheh

Decision

May I see the room?	Czy mogę zobaczyć pokój?	chi mogeh zobahchitsh pokooy
No, I don't like it.	Nie podoba mi się.	ñeh podobah mee syeh

FOR NUMBERS, see page 175

It's too...	Jest za...	yehst zah
cold/hot	zimny/gorący	zyeemni/gorontsi
dark/small	ciemny/mały	tshehmni/mahwi
noisy	hałaśliwy	hahwahsyleevi
No, that won't do at all.	Zupełnie mi nie odpowiada.	zoopehwñeh mee ñeh otpovyahdah
I asked for a room with a bath.	Prosiłem o pokój z łazienką.	prosyeewehm o pokooy zyehnkawng
Have you anything...?	Czy ma pan/pani jakiś...?	chi mah pahn/pahñee yahkeesy
better/bigger	lepszy/większy	lehpshi/vyehnkshi
cheaper/quieter	tańszy/bardziej cichy	tahñshi/bahrdzhay tsheehi
Have you a room with a better view?	Czy ma pan/pani pokój z ładniej-szym widokiem?	chi mah pahn/pahñee pokooy z wahdñayshim veedokehm
Could we have a cot for the baby/an extra bed for the child?	Proszę o dziecinne łóżko/dodatkowe łóżko dla dziecka?	prosheh o dzhehtsheenneh wooshko/dodahtkoveh wooshko dlah dzhehtskah
That's fine, I'll take it.	Dobrze. Biorę go.	dobzheh. byoreh go

HOTEL

Bills

These are usually paid upon departure. You pay for the room, not for the number of people occupying it. If you have a child and ask for an extra bed to be put in your room, a small charge will be made for this.

Tipping

A service charge (10%) is always included in the bill.

Though tipping is officially discouraged, gratuities, given discreetly, are welcomed. Tip the porter when he brings the bags to your room; tip the bellboy if he does any errands for you. Hold other tips till you check out.

FOR TIPPING, see also page 1

Registration

Upon arrival at a hotel you'll be asked to fill in a registration form *(karta zameldowania*—**kahr**tah zahmehldo**vah**ñah). It asks your name, home address, passport number. It's almost certain to carry an English translation. If it doesn't, ask the desk-clerk:

What does this mean?	**Co to znaczy?**	tso to **znah**chi

The desk-clerk will probably ask you for a passport. He may want to keep it for a while, even overnight. Don't worry—you'll get it back. The desk-clerk may want to ask you the following questions:

Proszę o paszport.	May I see your passport?
Proszę wypełnić kartę zameldowania.	Would you mind filling in this registration form?
Proszę tu podpisać.	Sign here, please.
Na jak długo pan/pani przyjechał?	How long will you be staying?

What's my room number?	**Jaki jest numer mojego pokoju?**	**yah**kee yehst **noo**mehr mo**yeh**go poko**yoo**
Will you have our bags sent up?	**Proszę przesłać nasze bagaże do pokoju.**	**pro**sheh **psheh**swahtsh **nah**sheh bah**gah**zheh do poko**yoo**
I'll take this briefcase with me.	**Tę teczkę wezmę sam.**	teh **tehch**keh **vehz**meh sahm

HOTEL

Service, please

Now that you're safely installed, meet some more of the hotel staff.

chambermaid	**pokojowa**	pokoyovah
manager	**kierownik**	kehrovñeek
head waiter	**kierownik sali**	kehrovñeek sahlee
waiter	**kelner**	kehlnehr

Call the members of the staff *pan* (pahn—Sir) or *pani* (**pah**ñee—Miss) when calling for service.

HOTEL SERVICE

General requirements

Please ask the chambermaid to come up.	**Proszę poprosić pokojową.**	prosheh poprosyeetsh pokoyovawng
Who is it?	**Kto tam?**	kto tahm
Just a minute.	**Chwileczkę.**	hfeelehchkeh
Come in!	**Proszę!**	prosheh
Is there a bath on this floor?	**Czy na tym piętrze jest łazienka?**	chi nah tim pyehnchsheh yehst wahzyehnkah
Where's the plug for a shaver?	**Gdzie jest kontakt do maszynki do golenia?**	gdzheh yehst kontahkt do mahshinkee do golehña
Please send up...	**Proszę przesłać...**	prosheh pshehswahtsh
two coffees	**dwie kawy**	dvyeh kahvi
a sandwich	**kanapkę**	kahnahpkeh
some soda water	**wodę sodową**	vodeh sodovawng
Can we have breakfast in our room?	**Czy możemy zjeść śniadanie w pokoju?**	chi mozhehmi z-yesytsh syñahdahñeh fpokoyoo
I'd like to leave these in your safe.	**Chciałbym to zostawić w depozycie.**	htshahwbim to zostahveetsh v dehpozitsheh
Can you find me a babysitter?	**Czy może pan/pani znaleźć mi opiekunkę dla dziecka?**	chi mozheh pahn/pahñee znahlehsytsh mee opyehkoonkeh do dzhehtskah

May I have a/an/some...	**Proszę...?**	prosheh
ashtray	**popielniczkę**	popyehlñeechkke
bath towel	**ręcznik kąpielowy**	**rehnch**ñeek kompyeh**lo**vi
extra blanket	**dodatkowy koc**	do**daht**kovi kots
more hangers	**więcej wieszaków**	vyehntsay vyeh**shah**koof
ice	**lód**	loot
needle and thread	**igłę i nitkę**	**eeg**weh ee **ñeet**keh
extra pillow	**dodatkową poduszkę**	dodaht**ko**vawng po**doosh**keh
pillow slips	**poszewki**	po**shehf**kee
reading lamp	**lampkę nocną**	**lahmp**keh **nots**nawng
soap	**mydło**	**mid**wo
writing paper	**papier do pisania**	**pah**pyehr do pee**sah**ñah
Where's the...?	**Gdzie jest...?**	gdzheh yehst
bathroom	**łazienka**	wa**zyehn**kah
beauty parlour	**gabinet kosmetyczny**	gah**bee**neht kosmeh**tich**ni
cocktail lounge	**barek**	**bah**rehk
dining room	**jadalnia**	yah**dahl**ñah
hairdresser's	**fryzjer**	**friz**-yehr
restaurant	**restauracja**	rehstah**wrah**tsyah
toilet	**toaleta**	twah**leh**tah

Breakfast

The Polish breakfast consists of tea or coffee (black or with cream), rolls and eggs or cold meats (sometimes jam but not marmalade). Tea isn't usually served with cold milk. Try it the Polish way. A Polish breakfast often begins with a milk soup. Cereals aren't common.

I'll have a/an/some...	**Proszę...**	prosheh
bacon and eggs	**jajka na bekonie**	**yigh**kah nah beh**koñ**eh
eggs	**jajka**	**yigh**kah
boiled egg	**jajko gotowane**	**yigh**ko goto**vah**neh
soft/medium/hard	**na miękko/średnio/na twardo**	nah **myehn**ko/**syrehd**ño/nah **tfahr**do
fried	**smażone**	sma**zho**neh
in a glass	**w szklance (po wiedeńsku)**	**fshklahn**tseh (po vyeh**dehñ**skoo)
scrambled	**jajecznicę**	yighyehch**ñeet**seh

fruit juice	**sok owocowy**	sok ovotsovi
grapefruit/orange	**grejpfrutowy/ pomarańczowy**	graypfrootovi/ pomahrahñchovi
pineapple/tomato	**ananasowy/ pomidorowy**	ahnahnahsovi/ pomeedorovi
ham and eggs	**jajka na szynce**	yighkah nah shintseh
kidneys	**cynaderki**	tsinahdehrkee
liver	**wątróbkę**	vontroopkeh
milk soup	**zupę mleczną**	zoopeh mlehchnawng
hot/cold	**gorącą/zimną**	gorontsawng/ zyeemnawng
omelet	**omlet**	omleht
sausages	**kiełbaski**	kehwbahskee
May I have some…?	**Proszę…**	prosheh
hot/cold milk	**gorące/zimne mleko**	gorontseh/zyeemneh mlehko
cream/sugar	**śmietankę/cukier**	symyehtahnkeh/tsookehr
more butter	**więcej masła**	vyehntsay mahswah
salt/pepper	**sól/pieprz**	sool/pyehpsh
coffee/tea	**kawę/herbatę**	kahveh/hehrbahteh
chocolate	**czekoladę**	chehkolahdeh
lemon/honey	**cytrynę/miód**	tsitrineh/myoot
Could you bring me a…?	**Proszę przynieść…?**	prosheh pshiñehsytsh
plate	**talerz**	tahlehsh
glass	**szklankę**	shklahnkeh
cup	**filiżankę**	feeleezhahnkeh
knife	**nóż**	noosh
fork	**widelec**	veedehlehts
spoon	**łyżkę**	wishkeh

Note: You'll find a great many other dishes listed in our guide "Eating Out" (pages 38–64). This should be consulted for your lunch and dinner menus.

Difficulties

The… doesn't work.	**… nie działa.**	ñeh dzhahwah
fan	**wentylator**	vehntilahtor
heating	**ogrzewanie**	ogzhehvahñeh
light	**światło**	syfyahtwo
tap (faucet)	**kurek**	koorehk
toilet	**ubikacja**	oobeekahtsyah

HOTEL SERVICE

The wash basin is blocked.	**Zlew jest zatkany.**	zlehf yehst zahtkahni
The window is jammed.	**Okno jest zablokowane.**	okno vehst zahblokovahneh
These aren't my shoes.	**To nie moje buty.**	to ñeh moyeh booti
This isn't my laundry.	**To nie moje rzeczy.**	to ñeh moyeh zhehchi
There's no hot water.	**Nie ma ciepłej wody.**	ñeh mah tshehpway vodi
I've lost my watch.	**Zgubiłem zegarek.**	zgoobeewehm zehgahrehk
I've left my key in my room.	**Zostawiłem klucz w pokoju.**	zostahveewehm klooch fpokoyoo
The ... is broken.	**... jest popsuta.**	yehst popsootah
lamp	**lampa**	lahmpa
shutter	**okiennica**	okehñ ñeetsah
plug	**kontakt jest popsuty**	kontahkt yehst popsooti
bulb	**żarówka jest przepalona**	zhahroofkah yehst pshehpahlonah
Can you get it fixed?	**Czy może pan to naprawić?**	chi mozheh pahn to nahprahveetsh

Telephone—Mail—Callers

Can you get me Cracow 12345?	**Proszę połączyć mnie z Krakowem numer 12345?**	prosheh powonchitsh mñeh skrahkovehm noomehr 12345
Did anyone telephone me?	**Czy ktoś do mnie dzwonił?**	chi ktosy do mñeh dzvoñeew
Operator, I've been cut off.	**Proszę pana/pani, przerwano mi.**	prosheh pahnah/pahñee pshehrvahno mee
Is there any mail for me?	**Czy jest dla mnie poczta?**	chi yehst dlah mñeh pochtah
Have you any stamps?	**Czy ma pan/pani znaczki?**	chi mah pahn/pahñee znahchkee
Are there any messages for me?	**Czy jest jakaś wiadomość dla mnie?**	chi yehst yahkahsy vyahdomosytsh dlah mñeh

FOR POST OFFICE, see page 137

Checking out

May I have my bill, please?	**Proszę rachunek.**	prosheh rahhoonehk
I'm leaving early tomorrow. Please have my bill ready.	**Wyjeżdżam jutro wcześnie rano. Proszę przygotować rachunek.**	viyehzhjahm yootro fchehsyñeh rahno. prosheh pshigotovahtsh rahhoonehk
We'll be checking out around noon/soon.	**Wyprowadzamy się koło południa/wkrótce.**	viprovahdzahmi syeh kowo powoodñah/fkrootseh
I must leave at once.	**Muszę wyjechać natychmiast.**	moosheh viyehhahtsh nahtihmyahst
You've made a mistake in this bill, I think.	**Sądzę, że pan/pani się pomylił.**	sondzeh zheh pahn/pahñee syeh pomileew
Can you get us a taxi?	**Czy może pan/pani sprowadzić nam taksówkę?**	chi mozheh pahn/pahñee sprovahdzheetsh nahm tahksoofkeh
When's the next... to Cracow?	**Kiedy jest następny... do Krakowa?**	kehdi yehst nahstehmpni... do krahkovah
bus/train/plane	**autobus/pociąg/samolot**	ahwtoboos/potshonk/sahmolot
Would you send someone to bring down our baggage?	**Czy może pan/pani posłać kogoś aby zniósł nam bagaże?**	chi mozheh pahn/pahñee poswahtsh kogosy ahbi zañoos nahm bahgahzheh
We're in a great hurry.	**Bardzo się spieszymy.**	bahrdzo syeh spyehshimi
Here's the forwarding address. You've my home address.	**Będziemy pod tym adresem. Pan/pani ma mój adres domowy.**	behñdzhehmi pot tim ahdrehsehm. pahn/pahñee mah mooy ahdrehs domovi
It's been a very enjoyable stay.	**Bardzo miło spędziliśmy tutaj czas.**	bahrdzo meewo spehñdzheeleesymi tootigh chahs
I hope we'll come again sometime.	**Mam nadzieję że jeszcze tu kiedyś przyjedziemy.**	mahm nahdzhehyeh zheh yehshcheh too kehdisy pshiyehdzhehmi

FOR TAXI, see page 27

HOTEL SERVICE

Eating out

There are various types of eating places and bars in Poland.

Bar
(bahr)

usually self-service where you can get food quickly and at low prices.

Bar mleczny
(bahr mlehchni)

a milk bar where you can get food of the breakfast and lunch type; no meat dishes are served; you can get soft drinks and milk shakes (known as *coctails*).

Coctail bar
(koktighl bahr)

be careful: this is a bar which serves milk shakes, ice-cream, cakes (cookies) and coffee. Unlike a milk bar it doesn't serve meals—but the cakes and ice-cream are recommended.

Kawiarnia
(kahvyahrñah)

a café; you can usually get breakfast in the morning. All cafés serve cakes (cookies), all types of drinks and occasionally hot dishes; in some cafés there is dancing in the evening.

Klub nocny
(kloop notsni)

a night-club.

Restauracja
(rehstahw-rahtsyah)

classified according to the standard of service and cuisine: *kat. S* (very high standard), *kat. I, kat. II, kat. III* (rare in big cities). Note that a low-category restaurant in a small town may serve excellent food at very modest prices.

Winiarnia
(veeñahrñah)

a wine house usually serving only wine.

In Poland service is always included (10% of the total). In night-clubs and cafés with dancing there's a minimum charge, often payable in advance.

The menu in high-category restaurants will be translated into English. It's always à la carte. Lunch is usually later than in Britain and America. Most restaurants serve hot dishes from 1 p.m. through to 11 p.m. or midnight. At night-clubs a variety of cold and some hot dishes are offered.

When you go into a *restauracja* or *kawiarnia* you'll see a cloak-room where you're expected to leave your topcoat. A small charge is usually made and advised for this service. The cloak-room attendant in most places sells cigarettes and matches. There isn't much to say to him, but he may say to you:

Razem?	Are you all together?
To pana/pani numerek.	Here's your disc.
Pan zapomniał zapłacić.	You've forgotten to pay.

It's also customary to leave the lavatory attendant a złoty or two. If there's no attendant there may be a sign up telling you the charge. Get to recognize the signs below:

DLA PAŃ/DAMSKI
LADIES

DLA PANÓW/MĘSKI
GENTLEMEN

TOALETA	LAVATORY
PŁATNA .. zł.	THE CHARGE IS .. ZŁOTY

EATING OUT

FOR TIPPING, see page 1

Eating habits

Polish cuisine owes much to its neighbouring countries, Russia, Germany and Hungary all having an influence on the style and favourite dishes. In the pages that follow we indicate some of the Polish specialities, but there are some dishes which, while not especially Polish, are particularly good in Poland. Smoked eel, for example, is a fine delicacy best sampled on the Baltic coast where it's caught; there are no mushrooms like Polish mushrooms; horseradish is excellent and very hot; steak tartare is always to be recommended, if you don't mind raw meat; then there is a wide selection of cold meats and ham; perhaps you thought that you didn't like tripe—if you try it in Poland you'll probably change your mind. And you must sample the most uniquely Polish dish, known as *bigos* (**bee**gos—sweet and sour cabbage cooked with a variety of meats).

Poles usually eat their main meal of the day sometime between 3 and 5 p.m. They generally have soup or a starter followed by one main dish, perhaps a dessert, and then coffee. Cheese isn't served as dessert. Except when eating out at hotels, it isn't usual to drink anything with the main meal; thus if you're staying at a boarding house or anywhere where a fixed meal is served, it won't usually be served with a drink. When eating out, however, beer, wine or vodka may be drunk; if you want something non-alcoholic, mineral water, coke, or some kind of juice will probably suit you.

In places which cater to tourists you'll always get milk or cream with your tea or coffee if you ask, but in some places it may just not be available, simply because in some regions of Poland people never take milk with tea or coffee. If milk in tea is a must for you, bring a few sachets of powdered milk with you to Poland.

When the waiter brings your food, he may say to you: *smacznego* (smahch**neh**go), which is the equivalent of "bon appetit". When people leave the table in Poland it's a custom to say *dziękuję*

EATING OUT

(dzhehn**koo**yeh—thank you) to one another. They aren't thanking the cook or their host, but thanking each other for eating together.

At the larger hotels you may have to wait some time for your meal. This is because it's being especially prepared for you and because, in any case, these hotels cater to the leisurely style of life. Service will be faster in lower-category restaurants and bars, if you're in a hurry.

Hungry?

I'm hungry/I'm thirsty.	**Jestem głodny/ Chce mi się pić.**	yehstehm **gwod**ni/htseh mee syeh peetsh
Can you recommend a good (and inexpensive) restaurant?	**Czy może pan/ pani polecić dobrą (i niedrogą) restaurację?**	chi **mo**zheh pahn/**pah**ñee po**leh**tsheetsh **do**brawng (ee ñeh**dro**gawng) rehstahw**rah**tsyeh

If you want to be sure of getting a table in well-known restaurants, it may be better to telephone in advance.

I'd like to reserve a table...	**Chciałbym zarezerwować stolik...**	**htshahw**bim zahrehzehr-**vo**vahtsh **sto**leek
for tonight	**na dzisiejszy wieczór**	nah dzhee**syay**shi **vyeh**choor
for tomorrow	**na jutro**	nah **yoo**tro
for... persons	**dla... osób**	dlah... **o**soop
for... o'clock	**na... godzinę**	nah... **go**dzheeneh

EATING OUT

FOR NUMBERS, see page 175

Asking and ordering

Good evening. I'd like a table for three.	Dobry wieczór. Proszę o stolik dla trzech osób.	dobri vyehchoor. prosheh o stoleek dlah chshehh osoop
Could we have a...?	Proszę stolik...	prosheh stoleek
table in the corner	w rogu	vrogoo
table by the window	przy oknie	pshi okňeh
table outside	na zewnątrz	nah zehvnontsh
table on the terrace	na tarasie	nah tahrahsyeh
quiet table somewhere	gdzieś w zaciszu	gdzhehsy vzahtsheeshoo
Where are the toilets?	Gdzie są toalety?	gdzheh sawng twahlehti
Can you serve me right away? I'm in a hurry.	Proszę o szybką obsługę. Spieszy mi się.	prosheh o shipkawng opswoogeh. spyehshi mee sye
What's the price of the fixed menu?	Ile kosztuje obiad firmowy?	eeleh koshtooyeh obyaht feermovi
Could we have a/an... please?	Proszę...	prosheh
ashtray	popielniczkę	popyehlňeechkeh
bottle of...	butelkę...	bootehlkeh
another chair	jeszcze jedno krzesło	yehshcheh yehdno kshehswo
glass	szklankę	shklahnkeh
glass of water	szklankę wody	shklahnkeh vodi
knife	nóż	noosh
napkin	serwetkę	sehrvehtkeh
plate	talerz	tahlehsh
spoon	łyżkę	wishkeh
tablecloth	obrus	obroos
toothpick	wykałaczkę	vikahwahchkeh
I'd like a/an/some...	Proszę...	prosheh
aperitif	aperitif	ahpehreeteef
appetizer	zakąskę	zahkonskeh
beer	piwo	peevo
beetroot	buraczki	boorahchkee
bread	chleb	hlehp
butter	masło	mahswo
cabbage	kapustę	kahpoosteh
carrots	marchewkę	mahrhehfkeh

FOR COMPLAINTS, see page 56

EATING OUT

cheese	ser	sehr
chips	frytki	fritkee
coffee	kawę	kahveh
dessert	deser	dehsehr
fish	rybę	ribeh
french fries	frytki	fritkee
fruit	owoce	ovotseh
game	dziczyznę	dzheechizneh
ice-cream	lody	lodi
ketchup	ketchup	kehchoop
lemon	cytrynę	tsitrineh
lettuce	sałatę	sahwahteh
meat	mięso	myehnso
mineral water	wodę mineralną	vodeh meenehrahlnawng
milk	mleko	mlehko
mustard	musztardę	mooshtahrdeh
olive oil	oliwę	oleeveh
peas	groszek	groshehk
pepper	pieprz	pyehpsh
potatoes	ziemniaki	zyehmñahkee
poultry	drób	droop
rice	ryż	rish
rolls	bułeczki	boohwehchkee
salad	sałatkę	sahwahtkeh
salt	sól	sool
sandwich	kanapkę	kahnahpkeh
seasoning	przyprawy	pshiprahvi
soup	zupę	zoopeh
spaghetti	spagetti	spahgehtee
spinach	szpinak	shpeenahk
sugar	cukier	tsookehr
tea	herbatę	hehrbahteh
vegetables	jarzynę	yahzhineh
vinegar	ocet	otseht
water	wodę	vodeh
wine	wino	veeno

What's on the menu?

Our menu has been presented according to courses. Under each heading you'll find an alphabetical list of dishes in Polish with their English equivalents. This list—which includes everyday items and special dishes—will enable you to make the most of a Polish menu.

Here's our guide to good eating and drinking. Turn to the course you want to start with.

	page	
Appetizers	45	**Zakąski**
Egg dishes and omelets	46	**Dania z jaj i omlety**
Soups	47	**Zupy**
Fish and seafood	48	**Dania rybne (Ryby)**
Meat	49	**Dania mięsne**
Game and fowl	51	**Dziczyzna i dania z drobiu**
Vegetables and seasonings	52	**Jarzyny**
Vegetarian dishes	53	**Dania jarskie (Bezmięsne)**
Fruits	53	**Owoce**
Dessert	54	**Desery**
Drinks	57	**Napoje**
Eating light—Snacks	64	**Zakąski i kanapki**

Obviously, you're not going to go through every course on the menu. If you've had enough, say:

Nothing more, thanks.	**To wszystko, dziękuję.**	to fshistko dzhehnkooyeh

EATING OUT

Appetizers—Starters

I would like an appetizer.	**Proszę o zakąskę.**	prosheh o zah**kon**skeh
What do you recommend?	**Co pan/pani poleca?**	tso pahn/**pah**ñee po**leh**tsah

drób w kokilce	droop fko**keel**tseh	poultry with white sauce
homary	ho**mah**ri	lobster
jajka	**yigh**kah	eggs
kalmary w majonezie	kahl**mah**ri vmigho**neh**zyeh	octopus in mayonnaise
kawior	**kah**vyor	caviar
kiełbasa	kehw**bah**sah	sausage
korki ze śledzia	**kor**kee zeh sy**leh**dzhah	marinated herring
krewetki	kreh**veht**kee	shrimp
łosoś wędzony	**wo**sosy veh**ndzo**ni	smoked salmon
ogórki konserwowe	o**goor**kee konsehr**vo**veh	gherkins (pickles)
oliwki	o**leef**kee	olives
omlet	**om**leht	omelet
ostrygi	os**tri**geh	oysters
pieczarki	pyeh**chahr**keh	mushrooms
pomidory	pome**edo**ri	tomatoes
przyprawy	pshi**prah**vi	seasonings
raki	**rah**kee	Polish lobster
rzodkiewki	zhot**kehf**kee	radishes
sałatka jarzynowa	sah**waht**kah yah**zhi**novah	vegetable salad
sałatka śledziowa	sah**waht**kah syleh**dzho**vah	herring salad
sandacz (w galarecie)	**sahn**dahch (vgahlah**reht**sheh)	perch (in aspic)
sardynki w oliwie	sahr**din**kee vo**lee**vyeh	sardines in oil
ser	sehr	cheese
sok owocowy	sok ovo**tso**vi	fruit juice
ananasowy	ahnahnah**so**vi	pineapple
pomarańczowy	pomahrah**ñcho**vi	orange
pomidorowy	pome**edo**rovi	tomato
szczupak (w galarecie)	shchoo**pahk** (vgahlah**reht**sheh)	pike (in aspic)
szparagi	shpah**rah**gee	asparagus tips
szynka	**shin**kah	ham
śledź w oleju	**sy**lehtsh vo**la**yoo	herring in oil
śledź w śmietanie	**sy**lehtsh fsymyeh**tah**ñeh	herring in sour cream

Polish appetizers

befsztyk tatarski	**behf**shtik tah**tahr**skee	raw meat, sardine, egg, onion, oil, cucumber, pepper, salt
bigos	**bee**gos	different kinds of sweet and sour cabbage with a variety of meats
flaki	**flah**kee	tripe with seasoning
forszmak	**forsh**mahk	veal in tomato sauce
karp na słodko z migdałami	kahrp nah **swot**ko z meegdah**wah**mee	carp in sweet almond sauce
naleśniki z kapustą i grzybami	nahleh**syñee**kee skah**poos**tawng ee gzhi**bah**mee	pancakes with cabbage and mushrooms
pasztet w auszpiku	**pahsh**teht v ahw**shpee**koo	paté in aspic
pieczarki w śmietanie	pyeh**chahr**kee fsymyeh**tah**ñeh	mushrooms in cream sauce
sandacz polski z jajkami	**sahn**dahch **pol**skee z yigh**kah**mee	Polish-style perch with eggs
węgorz w marynacie	**vehn**gozh v mahri**naht**sheh	eel in vegetable gelatin

Egg dishes and omelets

I would like an omelet.	**Proszę omlet.**	**pro**sheh **om**leht
jajecznicę z parmezanem	yighyeh**chñeet**seh s pahrmeh**zah**nehm	scrambled eggs with cheese
jajka sadzone na pomidorach	**yigh**kah sah**dzo**neh nah pomee**do**rahh	tomatoes and fried eggs
jajka na szynce	**yigh**kah nah **shin**tseh	ham and eggs
omlet z dżemem	**om**leht **zjeh**mehm	sweet omelet (with jam)
omlet z groszkiem	**om**leht **zgrosh**kehm	omelet with peas
omlet z grzybami	**om**leht zgzhi**bah**mee	mushroom omelet
omlet z szynką	**om**leht **sshin**kawng	ham omelet

Soups

I'd like some soup.	**Proszę zupę.**	prosheh zoopeh
What do you recommend?	**Którą pan/pani poleca?**	ktoorawng pahn/pahñee polehtsah
barszcz ukraiński	bahrshch ookraheeñskee	beetroot soup with various vegetables
bulion z diablotką	boolyon zdyahblotkawng	consommé with puff pastry
bulion z żółtkiem	boolyon zzhoowtkehm	consommé with egg
grochówka	grohoofkah	pea soup
grzybowa	gzhibovah	mushroom soup
jarzynowa	yahzhinovah	vegetable soup
kapuśniak	kahpoosyñahk	mixed (sweet and sour) cabbage soup
kartoflanka	kahrtoflahnkah	potato soup
ogórkowa	ogoorkovah	salt-cucumber soup
pomidorowa	pomeedorovah	tomato soup
rosół	rosoow	broth
rybna	ribnah	fish soup
szczawiowa	shchahvyovah	sorrel soup

Polish soups

barszcz czerwony	bahrshch chehrvoni	beetroot soup
barszcz czysty	bahrshch chisti	clear beetroot soup
barszcz zabielany	bahrshch zahbeeehlahni	beetroot soup with sour cream
chłodnik	hwodñeek	cold beetroot soup with cream and fresh vegetables
żurek	zhoorehk	sour rye flour soup, usually with cream

EATING OUT

Salads

Note that a salad isn't served as a main dish. You may have salad as a starter or as a side dish.

Fish and seafood

I'd like some fish.	Proszę rybę.	prosheh ribeh
What kind of seafood have you got?	Jakie są dania z ryb?	yahkeh sawng dahñah zrip

dorsz	dorsh	cod
flądra	flondrah	flounder
halibut	hahleeboot	halibut
homar	homahr	lobster
kalmary	kahlmahri	squid
karmazyn	kahrmahzin	haddock
karp	kahrp	carp
krewetki	krehvehtkee	shrimp
leszcz	lehshch	bream
lin	leen	tench
łosoś	wososy	salmon
makrela	mahkrehlah	mackerel
ostrygi	ostrigee	oysters
pstrąg	pstronk	trout
rak	rahk	Polish lobster
sandacz	sahndach	perch
sardynki	sahrdinkee	sardines
sielawa	syehlahvah	bleak
sola	solah	sole
szczupak	shchoopahk	pike
śledź	sylehtsh	herring
tuńczyk	tooñchik	tunny (tuna)
węgorz	vehngosh	eel

EATING OUT

There are many ways of preparing fish. Here are the Polish translations of the ways you may want it served.

baked	**zapiekana**	zahpyehkahnah
fried	**smażona**	smahzhonah
grilled	**z rusztu**	zrooshtoo
jellied	**w galarecie**	vgahlahrehtsheh
marinated	**marynowana**	mahrinovahnah
poached	**z wody**	zvodi
smoked	**wędzona**	vehndzonah
steamed	**duszona**	dooshonah

Meat

What kind of meat do you have?	Jakie rodzaje mięs ma pan/pani?	yahkeh rodzahyeh myehns mah pahn/pahñee
I'd like some...	Proszę...	prosheh
beef	wołowinę	vowoveeneh
pork	wieprzowinę	vyehpshoveeneh
veal	cielęcinę	tshehlehntsheeneh

Beef

befsztyk	behfshtik	beef steak
brisol	brizol	grilled beef steak
kotlet mielony	kotleht myehloni	minced beef
ozór wołowy	ozoor vowovi	tongue
pieczeń wołową	pyehchehñ vowovawng	roast beef
polędwicę po angielsku	polehndveetseh po ahngehlskoo	roast fillet of beef
rosbef	rozbehf	roast beef
rumsztyk	roomshtik	rumpsteak
stek	stehk	steak
sztukę mięsa	shtookeh myehnsa	boiled beef

Pork

eskalop schabowy	ehskahlop s-hahbovi	loin of pork
pieczeń wieprzową	pyehchehñ vyehpshovawng	roast pork
schab pieczony	s-hahp pyehchoni	roast loin of pork

Veal

cynaderki	tsinahdehrkee	kidneys
filet cielęcy	feeleht tshehlehntsi	veal scallop
mostek cielęcy	mostehk tshehlehntsi	veal brisket
móżdżek	moozhjehk	calf's brains
pieczeń cielęcą	pyehchehñ tshehlehntsawng	roast veal
sznycel cielęcy	shnitsehl tshehlehntsi	veal scallop
wątróbkę	vontroopkeh	liver
ozorki cielęce	ozorkee tshehlehntseh	veal tongue

EATING OUT

Other meat dishes

flaki	flahkee	tripe with seasoning
gulasz	goolahsh	goulash
kiełbasę na gorąco	kehwbahseh nah gorontso	hot sausage
pieczeń baranią	pyehchehn bahrahñawng	roast mutton
szaszłyk	shahshwik	mutton shashlik
szynkę	shinkeh	ham
gotowaną	gotovahnawng	cooked
wędzoną	vehndzonawng	smoked

How do you like your meat?

barbecued	**z rusztu**	**z**rooshtoo
braised	**gotowane**	goto**vah**neh
fried	**smażone**	smah**zh**oneh
roast	**pieczone**	**pyeh**choneh
stewed	**duszone**	**doo**shoneh
stuffed	**faszerowane**	fahshehro**vah**neh
rare	**po angielsku**	po ahn**gehl**skoo
medium	**średnio**	**syrehd**ño
	wysmażone	vismah**zh**oneh
well-done	**mocno**	**mots**no
	wysmażone	vismah**zh**oneh

Polish specialities

We recommend you to have...	**Polecamy...**	poleh**tsah**mi
golonkę	golonkeh	boiled leg of pork
kotlet schabowy z kapustą	kotleht s-hahbovi skah**poo**stawng	pork chop with cabbage
szaszłyk z polędwicy	shahshwik spolehnd**vee**tsi	barbecued chunks of beef on a skewer with onions

Game and fowl

I'd like some game.	**Proszę dziczyznę.**	prosheh dzheechizneh
What poultry dishes do you serve?	**Jakie są dania z drobiu?**	yahkeh sawng dahñah zdrobyoo
indyk	eendik	turkey
kaczka pieczona	kahchkah pyehchonah	roast duck
kotlet de volaille	kotleht deh volay	breaded fried chicken
kurczę	koorcheh	chicken
kuropatwy	kooropahtfi	partridge
rizotto z drobiu	reezotto zdrobyoo	chicken and rice casserole
przepiórki	pshehpyoorkee	quail
zając	zahyonts	hare

Game and fowl dishes

bażant pieczony	bahzhahnt pyehchoni	broiled pheasant
comber sarni	tsombehr sahrñee	loin of deer
gęś pieczona	gehñsy pyehchonah	roast goose
kaczka z jabłkami	kahchkah zjahpkahmee	duck stuffed with apples
kura w potrawce	koorah fpotrahftseh	fricassee of chicken
kura w rosole	koorah vrosoleh	leg of chicken in broth
kurczę po polsku	koorcheh po polskoo	roast chicken stuffed with liver and white bread
pieczeń z dzika	pyehchehñ zdzheekah	roast wild boar
zając w śmietanie	zahyonts fsymyehtahñeh	roast hare in cream

Vegetables and seasonings

What vegetables do you recommend?	Jakie jarzyny pan/pani poleca?	yahkeh yahzhini pahn/ pahñee polehtsah
I prefer some salad.	Wolę sałatkę.	voleh sahwahtkeh

brukiew	brookehf	turnips
brukselka	brooksehlkah	brussels sprouts
buraczki	boorahchkee	beet(root)
cebula	tsehboolah	onions
chrzan	hshahn	horseradish
cykoria	tsikoryah	endives
czosnek	chosnehk	garlic
fasola	fahsolah	beans
frytki	fritkee	chips (french fries)
groszek	groshehk	peas
grzyby	gzhibi	mushrooms
kalafior	kahlahfyor	cauliflower
kapusta	kahpoostah	cabbage
karczochy	kahrchohi	artichokes
koperek	kopehrehk	dill
kukurydza	kookooridzah	corn on the cob
marchewka	mahrhehfkah	carrots
mizeria	meezehryah	chopped cucumbers with cream
ogórek	ogoorehk	cucumber
ogórek kiszony	ogoorehk keeshoni	pickled cucumber
ogórki konserwowe	ogoorkee konsehrvoveh	gherkins
pieprz	pyehpsh	pepper
pietruszka	pyehtrooshkah	parsley
pomidory	pomeedori	tomatoes
pory	pori	leeks
ryż	rish	rice
rzodkiewki	zhotkehfkee	radishes
sałata	sahwahtah	lettuce
sałatka mieszana	sahwahtkah myehshahnah	mixed vegetables
selery	sehlehri	celery
szczypiorek	shchipyorehk	chives
szparagi	shpahrahgee	asparagus (tips)
szpinak	shpeenahk	spinach
trufle	troofleh	truffles
tymianek	timyahnehk	thyme
ziemniaki	zyehmñahkee	potatoes

EATING OUT

Vegetarian dishes

The typical Polish dishes are what you'll find in a *bar mleczny*.
They're usually available in restaurants as well. Note that some
contain a little meat.

bukiet z jarzyn	bookeht zyahzhin	various vegetables
fasolka po bretońsku	fahsolkah po brehtońskoo	beans in tomato sauce
knedle	knehdleh	dumplings with plums
kopytka	kopitkah	potato dumplings
leniwe pierogi	lehñeeveh pyehrogee	dumplings with white cheese
makaron z jajkami	mahkahron zyighkahmee	macaroni with fried eggs
naleśniki	nahlenhsyñeekee	pancakes
z marmoladą	zmahrmolahdawng	with jam
z serem	ssehrehm	with white cheese
pieczarki z patelni	pyehchahrkee spahtehlñee	fried mushrooms
pierogi z jagodami	pyehrogee zyahgodahmee	dumplings with bilberries
pierogi z mięsem	pyehrogee zmyehnsehm	meat dumplings
pierogi z wiśniami	pyehrogee zveesyñahmee	dumplings with cherries
placki ziemniaczane	plahtskee zyehmñahchahneh	potato pancakes
pyzy	pizi	a kind of dumpling

Fruit

Do you have fresh fruit?	**Czy są świeże owoce?**	chi sawng syfehzheh ovotseh
agrest	ahgrehst	gooseberries
ananas	ahnahnahs	pineapple
arbuz	ahrboos	watermelon
banany	bahnahni	bananas
brzoskwinie	bzhoskfeeñeh	peaches
cytryna	tsitrinah	lemon
czarne jagody	chahrneh yahgodi	blackberries
czereśnie	chehrehsyñeh	cherries
daktyle	dahktileh	dates
dynia	diñah	pumpkin
figi	feegee	figs

grejpfrut	graypfroot	grapefruit
gruszki	grooshkee	pears
jabłka	yahpkah	apples
kasztany	kahshtahni	chestnuts
maliny	mahleeni	raspberries
mandarynki	mahndahrinkee	tangerines
melon	mehlon	melon
migdały	meegdahwi	almonds
morele	morehleh	apricots
oliwki	oleefkee	olives
orzechy włoskie	ozhehhi vwoskeh	walnuts
orzeszki laskowe	ozhehshkee lahskoveh	hazelnuts
pomarańcze	pomahrahñcheh	oranges
porzeczki	pozhehchkee	currants
poziomki	pozyomkee	wild strawberries
rabarbar	rahbahrbahr	rhubarb
renklody	rehnglodi	greengage
rodzynki	rodzinkee	raisins
śliwki	syleefkee	plums
sułtanki	soowtahnkee	sultanas
suszone śliwki	sooshoneh syleefkee	prunes
truskawki	trooskahfkee	strawberries
winogrona	veenogronah	grapes
żurawiny	zhoorahveeni	cranberries

Dessert

If you've survived all the courses on the menu, you may want
to say:

I'd like a dessert, please.	**Proszę o deser.**	prosheh o dehsehr
Something light, please.	**Coś lekkiego proszę.**	tsosy lehkkehgo prosheh
Just a small portion.	**Małą porcję.**	mahwawng portsyeh
Nothing more, thanks.	**To wszystko, dziękuję.**	to fshistko dzhehnkooyeh

If you aren't sure what to order, ask the waiter:

What have you for dessert?	**Co można zjeść na deser?**	tso mozhnah zyehsytsh nah dehsehr

What do you recommend?	Co pan/pani poleca?	tso pahn/**pah**ñee po**leh**tsah
ananas	ahnahnahs	pineapple
bita śmietana z rodzynkami	**bee**tah symyeh**tah**nah zrodzin**kah**mee	whipped cream with sultanas
budyń	**boo**diñ	milk pudding
ciastko	tshahstko	cake
galaretka	gahlah**reht**kah	jelly
gruszka w czekoladzie	**groosh**kah fchehko**lah**dzheh	pears in chocolate sauce
herbatniki	hehrbaht**ñee**kee	biscuits (cookies)
kompot	kompot	stewed fruit
krem z czekoladą	krehm schehko**lah**dawng	cream with chocolate
lody	lodi	ice-cream
bakaliowe	bahkahl**yo**veh	tutti-frutti
czekoladowe	chehkolah**do**veh	chocolate
mieszane	myeh**shah**neh	mixed
truskawkowe	trooskahf**ko**veh	strawberry
waniliowe	vahñeel**yo**veh	vanilla
melba	**mehl**bah	ice-cream with whipped cream and different kinds of fruits
migdały w soli	meeg**dah**wi fsolee	salted almonds
sałatka z pomarańczy	sah**wah**tkah spomah**rah**ñchi	orange salad
sernik	**sehr**ñeek	cheese cake
sękacz	**sehn**kahch	fancy layer cake
tort czekoladowy	tort chehkolah**do**vi	chocolate cake

You'll notice that cheese doesn't appear on our dessert list. It's not eaten after the main course in Poland. A meal usually ends with coffee.

A coffee, please.	**Proszę kawę.**	**pro**sheh **kah**veh
A coffee with cream.	**Proszę kawę ze śmietanką.**	**pro**sheh **kah**veh zeh symyeh**tahn**kawng
Some tea, please.	**Proszę herbatę.**	**pro**sheh hehr**bah**teh

That's the end of our Polish menu. For wine and other drinks, see the next pages. But after the feast comes…

EATING OUT

The bill (check)

May I have the bill (check), please?	Proszę o rachunek.	prosheh o rahhoonehk
Haven't you made a mistake?	Czy pan/pani się nie pomylił?	chi pahn/pahñee syeh ñeh pomileew
Is everything included?	Czy rachunek obejmuje wszystko?	chi rahhoonehk obaymooyeh fshistko
Do you accept traveller's cheques?	Czy pan/pani przyjmuje czeki podróżne?	chi pahn/pahñee pshiymooyeh chehkee podroozhneh
Thank you, this is for you.	Dziękuję, to dla pana/pani.	dzhehnkooyeh to dlah pahnah/pahñee
Keep the change.	Reszty nie trzeba.	rehshti ñeh chshehbah
That was a very good meal. We enjoyed it, thank you.	Jedzenie było bardzo dobre. Smakowało nam. Dziękuję.	yehdzehñeh biwo bahrdzo dobreh. smahkovahwo nahm. dzhehnkooyeh
We'll come again sometime.	Przyjdziemy tu jeszcze kiedyś.	pshiydzhehmi too yehshchheh kehdisy

Complaints

But perhaps you'll have something to complain about...

There's a draught (draft) here. Could you give us another table?	Tu jest przeciąg. Może pan/pani dać inny stolik?	too yehst pshehtshonk mozheh nahm pahn/pahñee dahtsh eenni stoleek
That's not what I ordered. I asked for...	Tego nie zamawiałem. Prosiłem o...	tehgo ñeh zahmahvyahwehm. prosyeewehm o
May I change this?	Czy mogę to zamienić?	chi mogeh to zahmyehñeetsh
The meat is...	Mięso jest...	myehnso yehst
overdone	przesmażone	pshehsmahzhoneh
underdone	niedosmażone	ñehdosmahzhoneh
too tough	za twarde	zahtfahrdeh

EATING OUT

Drinks

Alcoholic drinks

Polish drinking habits vary considerably from British or American customs, and while the bigger hotels cater to the foreign tourist, it'll be useful and interesting for you to know how the Poles tackle this important area of life. A word of warning: vodka is the national speciality and they know how to handle it. Don't try to outdrink a Pole.

You'll be told that something to eat must be taken with alcohol, and in some bars they'll only serve vodka with some kind of snack. Conversely, there are some foods that simply must be taken with alcohol: smoked eel must have vodka to swim in your stomach.

In this section we'll be covering all the most common drinks in Poland and indicating when they are usually drunk.

Beer

While you're in Poland you may have the chance of sampling Czech or German beer, both of which are deservedly famous, but Polish beer is also good and strong. *Żywiec* (**zhi**vyehts) beer is particularly recommended.

Beer is often taken with meals in Poland or it can be drunk in the *kawiarnia* (kah**vyahr**ñah) at any time of the day. There are a few establishments known as *piwiarnia* (pee**vyahr**ñah—from *piwo*, beer) exclusively devoted to the business of drinking beer. As in Britain, beer is usually drunk at room temperature, but the larger hotels offer cold beer.

A (cold) beer, please.	**Proszę (zimne) piwo.**	prosheh (zyeemneh) peevo
Two/Three/Four beers, please.	**Proszę dwie/trzy/ cztery butelki piwa.**	prosheh dvyeh/chshi/ chtehri bootehlkee peevah

| One more glass, please. | Proszę jeszcze jedną szklankę. | prosheh yeshcheh yehdnawng shklahnkeh |
| Do you have any German/Czech beer? | Czy ma pan/pani piwo niemieckie/czeskie? | chi mah pahn/pahñee peevo ñehmyehtskeh/chehskeh |

Wine

Almost all wines are imported from Hungary, Bulgaria, Romania and Yugoslavia. French and Spanish wines are available but they tend to be expensive. You should take the opportunity of trying Russian champagne, *Szampan* (**shahm**pahn), and Hungarian white *Tokaj* (**to**kigh). If you ask for a white wine, you'l probably be offered a *Rizling* (**riz**leenk), if you ask for a red you may be offered the famous Bull's Blood–*Egri Bikave* (**eh**gree bee**kah**vehr)—from Hungary. If you're in Poland in th cold wheather there's nothing like a glass of mulled red wine which is sold at many establishments, particularly in the mountains.

Wine is, of course, drunk with food. It's usually available by th glass in the *kawiarnia* (kah**vyahr**ñah), but if you're really inter ested in drinking wine, ask someone to direct you to a *winiarni* (vee**ñahr**ñah), a wine drinking cellar. These are usually livel places with a good atmosphere. There are several well worth visit around the Old Town in Warsaw.

I'd like a bottle/glass of...	Proszę butelkę/lampkę...	prosheh bootehlkeh/lahmpkeh
two glasses of...	dwie lampki...	dvyeh lahmpkee
I'd like something...	Proszę jakieś...	prosheh yahkehsy
sweet/sparkling/dry	słodkie/musujące/wytrawne wino	swotkeh/moosooyontseh/vitrahvneh veeno
I want a bottle of...	Proszę butelkę...	prosheh bootehlkeh
white wine	białego wina	byahwehgo veenah
red wine	czerwonego wina	chehrvonehgo veenah
champagne	szampana	shahmpahnah

I don't want anything too sweet.	**Niezbyt słodkie, proszę.**	nehzbit swotkeh prosheh
How much is a bottle of...?	**Ile kosztuje butelka...?**	eeleh koshtooyeh bootehlkah
That's too expensive.	**To za drogo.**	to zah drogo
Haven't you anything cheaper?	**Czy nie ma pan/ pani nic tańszego?**	chi ñeh mah pahn/pahñee ñeets tahñshehgo
What country does it come from?	**Skąd pochodzi to wino?**	skont pohodzhee to veeno
I don't want French wine.	**Nie chcę wina francuskiego.**	ñeh htseh veenah frahntsooskehgo

If you enjoyed the wine, you may want to say:

Bring me another glass/bottle, please.	**Proszę jeszcze jedną lampkę/ butelkę.**	prosheh yehshcheh yehdnawng lahmpkeh/ bootehlkeh
What is the name of this wine?	**Jak się nazywa to wino?**	yahk syeh nahzivah to veeno

dry	**wytrawne**	vitrahvneh
half-dry	**półwytrawne**	poowvitrahvneh
sweet	**słodkie**	swotkeh
white	**białe**	byahweh
red	**czerwone**	chehrvoneh
sparkling	**musujące**	moosooyontseh
chilled	**zimne**	zyeemneh
at room temperature	**w temperaturze pokojowej**	ftehmpehrahtoozheh pokoyovay
mulled	**grzane**	gzhahneh

EATING OUT

Vodka

Get rid of the idea that vodka is a colourless and tasteless spirit or that it's only a Russian drink. There are many different kinds, colours and flavours of Polish vodka. At a typical Polish meal vodka and just vodka is drunk. It's always drunk neat (straight), and it's a tradition that a glass is downed in one gulp—but go easy on this. Some people, as well as ordering vodka, will order some bottles of mineral water. You've a separate glass for the mineral water. You never dilute the vodka.

It's best to drink vodka chilled. Don't be surprised when you go to the bar of your hotel hoping to sample the local speciality: you'll see a wide variety of drinks that you know on the shelves, but no vodka. It's being kept in the fridge, where it should be. Here is a list of some of the better known vodkas:

Cytrynówka (tsitri**noof**kah)	Lemon-flavoured vodka
Jarzębiak (jah**zhehm**byahk)	Vodka flavoured with rowanberries, a very popular one
Myśliwska (misy**leef**skah)	Hunter's vodka; it has a flavour rather like gin.
Pieprzówka (pyehp**shoof**kah)	Pepper-flavoured vodka, believe it or not
Soplica (sop**leet**sah)	A dry and very fine golden-coloured vodka
Wiśniówka (veesy**ñoof**kah)	Cherry-flavoured vodka, rather sweet
Wódka czysta (**voot**kah **chist**ah)	The classical clear vodka, ideal with a meal
Wyborowa (vibo**ro**vah)	The best clear vodka
Żubrówka (zhoob**roof**kah)	Bison vodka, known by this name because it's flavoured with the grass on which the bison feeds. If you look in the bottle you'll see a blade of this grass.
Żytnia (**zhit**ñah)	Top-quality clear vodka

As well as the commercially-produced brands there's an almost infinite variety of fruit-flavoured vodkas. Every Polish family has its own special recipes, but you'll have to make friends with the locals if you want to try these.

In the larger hotels you'll be able to order your favourite aperitifs but ask for them in English: they all go by their English names. But a word here about brandy and two or three other Polish specialities will be useful.

Polish brandy is known as *winiak* (**vee**ñahk). All foreign brandies are known as cognacs—*koniaki* (koñahkee)—so ask for what you want. If you want a cognac specify if you want French or some other type. Georgian brandy is recommended.

Mead *(miód*—myoot)—a fermented beverage of water, honey, malt and yeast—is a very Polish drink and is particularly good if mulled with spices. There are special places for drinking mead: a famous cellar under the clock tower in Cracow and a bar in Piękna Street in Warsaw. Mead tends to go to your legs rather than your head, so be careful when you stand up. You might also like to try the liqueur made from mead. It's called *Krupnik* (**kroop**ñeek) and provides a warm lining on a cold day.

Polish *Śliwowica* (syleevo**vee**tsah) is justly famous. It's a spirit distilled from plums and is stronger than any vodka.

I'd like a glass of..., please.	**Proszę o lampkę...**	prosheh o **lahm**pkeh
Could I have some soda water?	**Proszę o wodę sodową.**	prosheh o **vo**deh so**do**vawng
Get me some ice, please.	**Proszę o lód.**	prosheh o loot
Some more ice, please.	**Proszę trochę więcej lodu.**	prosheh **tro**heh **vyehn**tsay **lo**doo
I want it neat (straight).	**Bez lodu proszę.**	behz **lo**doo **pro**sheh

EATING OUT

We'd like some mulled mead.	**Proszę grzany miód.**	prosheh **gzhah**ni myoot
Georgian brandy	**koniak gruziński**	koñahk groozyeeñskee
French cognac	**koniak francuski**	koñahk frahntsooskee
What liqueurs do you have?	**Jakie likiery ma pan/pani?**	yahkeh leekehri mah pahn/pahñee
One vodka, please.	**Proszę kieliszek wódki.**	prosheh kehleeshehk vootkee
Two vodkas.	**Dwa kieliszki wódki.**	dvah kehleeshkee vootkee
What do you recommend?	**Co pan/pani poleca?**	tso pahn/pahñee polehtsah

Remember, if no translation of your favourite drink appear here, ask for it in English. If the bar has the drink, you'll b understood. One final word of warning: it's an offence to driv in Poland with even a minimum content of alcohol in your bloo

NA ZDROWIE!
(nahzdrovyeh)
CHEERS!

Other beverages

As in many European countries, a lot of time is spent in cafés in Poland, just sipping a coffee or something else, nibbling at cake and watching the world go by. Coffee in Poland is served strong and black. You can ask for milk, but you'll probably be offered whipped cream instead, which is much better, of course. As a special treat you should try coffee in the old Polish style, which means coffee with lots of cream, a glass of something strong and cinnamon added. Another speciality is natural black-currant juice. On a hot day, put a little soda water and ice in it for a real thirst quencher. A *coctail* (**kok**tighl—milk shake) is a popular refresher.

I'd like a...	Proszę...	prosheh
Have you any...?	Czy jest...?	chi yehst
chocolate	gorąca czekolada	gorontsah chehkolahdah
coffee	kawa	kahvah
small coffee	mała	mahwah
large coffee	duża	doozhah
iced coffee	mrożona	mrozhonah
coffee with cream	kawa ze	kahvah zeh
	śmietanką	symyehtahnkawng
old-Polish style	po staropolsku	po stahropolskoo
fruit juice	sok owocowy	sok ovotsovi
apple	jabłkowy	yahpkovi
black-currant	z czarnej	schahrnay pozhehchkee
	porzeczki	
grapefruit	grejpfrutowy	graypfrootovi
orange	pomarańczowy	pomahrahñchovi
pineapple	ananasowy	ahnahnahsovi
tomato	pomidorowy	pomeedorovi
milk	mleko	mlehko
sour milk	kwaśne mleko	kfahsyneh mlehko
milk shake	coctail mleczny	koktighl mlehchni
blackberry	jagodowy	yahgodovi
apple	jabłkowy	yahpkovi
mineral water	woda mineralna	vodah meenehrahlnah
soda water	woda sodowa	vodah sodovah
tea	herbata	hehrbahtah
with lemon	z cytryną	stsitrinawng
tonic water	tonic	toñeek
yoghurt	jogurt	yogoort

Eating light—Snacks

In the *kawiarnia* (kah**vyahr**ñah) there'll be a variety of light snacks to choose from. Some cafés are famous for their ice-cream. Others have a super collection of cakes and pastries.

I'll have one of those, please.	**Proszę to.**	prosheh to
Give me two of these and one of those.	**Proszę dwa takie i jedno takie.**	prosheh dvah tahkeh ee yehdno tahkeh
to the left/to the right	**na lewo/na prawo**	nah lehvo/nah prahvo
above/below	**wyżej/niżej**	vizhay/ñeezhay
Give me a/an/some…, please.	**Proszę…**	prosheh
biscuits (cookies)	**herbatniki**	hehrbahtñeekee
bread	**chleb**	hlehp
(white) bread	**bułkę**	boowkeh
butter	**masło**	mahswo
cake	**ciastko**	tshahstko
candy	**cukierki**	tsookehrkee
frankfurters	**parówki**	pahroofkee
ice-cream	**lody**	lodi
roll	**bułeczkę**	boowehchkeh
salad	**sałatkę**	sahwahtkeh
sandwich	**kanapkę**	kahnahpkeh
with cheese	**z serem**	ssehrehm
with ham	**z szynką**	shshinkawng
toast	**grzankę**	gzhahnkeh
sweets	**cukierki**	tsookehrkee
waffles	**wafelki**	vahfehlkee

garlic	**czosnek**	chosnehk
mustard	**musztardę**	mooshtahrdeh
pepper	**pieprz**	pyehpsh
salt	**sól**	sool
vinegar	**ocet**	otseht

How much is that?	**Ile to kosztuje?**	eeleh to koshtooyeh

EATING OUT

Travelling around

Plane

Very brief—because at any airport you're sure to find someone who speaks English. But here are a few useful expressions you may want to know…

Do you speak English?	Czy pan/pani mówi po angielsku?	chi pahn/**pah**ñee **moo**vi po ahn**gehl**skoo
Is there a flight to Cracow?	Czy jest lot do Krakowa?	chi yest lot do krah**ko**vah
When's the next plane to Gdańsk?	Kiedy jest następny samolot do Gdańska?	**keh**di yehst nahs**tehmp**ni sah**mo**lot do **gdah**ñskah
Can I make a connection to Szczecin?	Czy będę miał połączenie do Szczecina?	chi **behn**deh myahw powon**cheh**ñeh do shcheh**tsee**nah
I'd like a ticket to Wrocław.	Proszę bilet do Wrocławia.	**pro**sheh **bee**leht to vrots**wahv**yah
What's the fare to Gdańsk?	Ile kosztuje bilet do Gdańska?	**ee**leh kosh**too**yeh **bee**leht do **gdah**ñskah
What time does the plane take off?	O której godzinie odlatuje samolot?	o **ktoo**ray go**dzhee**ñeh odlah**too**yeh sah**mo**lot
What time do I have to check in?	O której godzinie mam się zgłosić?	o **ktoo**ray go**dzhee**ñeh mahm syeh **zgwo**syeetsh
What's the flight number?	Jaki jest numer lotu?	**yah**kee yehst **noo**mehr **lo**too
What time do we arrive?	O której godzinie przylatujemy?	o **ktoo**ray go**dzhee**ñeh pshilah**too**yehmi

PRZYLOT	ODLOT
ARRIVAL	DEPARTURE

Trains

There's a good network of railways in Poland, and even if the train isn't as fast as the plane, it's probably more reliable under severe weather conditions.

All main-line trains have first- and second-class compartments and you'll have a dining car or buffet car on all long-distance trains. If you want to make the most of your time in Poland you may well want to take a night sleeper to travel from one end of the country to the other.

When deciding which train to catch you should check whether the one you have in mind is an express *(pociąg ekspresowy—* **po**tshonk ehksprehsovi), a fast *(prociąg pospieszny—* **po**tshonk pos**pyeh**shni) or a local train *(pociąg osobowy—* **po**tshonk oso**bo**vi). You'll have to have a reservation for an express train. They're optional for fast trains. Get your ticket and reservation in advance from an Orbis office or from a Polres office—an office which deals with train tickets and reservations. On the day before you're travelling or the day itself you can buy your ticket at the station. There's a small fee for seat reservation, and tickets on fast and express trains are slightly more expensive than on local trains. Remember that if you're travelling at a busy time and you're told at the Orbis office that there are no tickets for a particular train, you may very well be able to purchase such a ticket at the station. Return (roundtrip) tickets are generally not available. For international tickets go to the Orbis office. You'll have to pay for these in foreign currency.

To the railway station

Where's the railway station?	**Gdzie jest stacja kolejowa?**	gdzheh yehst **stah**tsyah koleh**yo**vah
Taxi, please!	**Taksówka!**	tahk**soof**kah
Take me to the railway station.	**Proszę mnie zawieźć na stację.**	**pro**sheh mńeh **zah**vyesytsh nah **stah**tsyeh
What's the fare?	**Ile płacę?**	**ee**leh **pwah**tseh

Tickets

Where's the...?	Gdzie jest...?	gdzheh yehst
information office	informacja	eenformahtsyah
reservation office	biuro rezerwacji biletów	byooro rehzehrvahtsyee beelehtoof
ticket office	kasa biletowa	kahsah beelehtovah
I want a ticket to Cracow, second-class, on a...	Proszę bilet do Krakowa drugiej klasy...	prosheh beeleht do krahkovah droogay klahsi
fast train	na pociąg pospieszny	nah potshonk pospyehshni
express train	na pociąg ekspresowy	nah potshonk ehksprehsovi
local train	na pociąg osobowy	nah potshonk osobovi
I'd like two singles to Gdynia.	Proszę dwa bilety do Gdyni.	prosheh dvah beelehti do gdiñee
How much is the fare to Zakopane?	Ile kosztuje bilet do Zakopanego?	eeleh koshtooyeh beeleht do zahkopahnehgo
Is it half price for a child? He's eleven.	Czy jest pięćdziesiąt procent zniżki dla dziecka? Ma jedenaście lat.	chi yehst pyehñdzhehsyont protsehnt zñeeshkee dlah dzhehtskah? mah yehdehnahsytsheh laht

Note: Children up to the age of four travel free; children under ten pay half fare.

TRAVELLING AROUND

Possible answers

Pierwsza czy druga klasa?	First or second class?
W jedną stronę czy powrotny?	Single or return (one-way or roundtrip)?
Dla dzieci do dziesięciu lat jest pięćdziesiąt procent zniżki.	It's half price up to the age of ten.
Musi pan/pani zapłacić za pełny bilet.	You'll have to pay full fare.

FOR TAXI, see page 27

68

Further enquiries

Is it a through train?	**Czy to jest pociąg bezpośredni?**	chi to yehst **potshonk** behsposyrehdñee
Does this train stop at Malbork?	**Czy ten pociąg zatrzymuje się w Malborku?**	chi tehn **potshonk** zahchshimooyeh syeh vmahlborkoo
When is the... train to Gdynia?	**Kiedy jest... pociąg do Gdyni?**	kehdi yehst... **potshonk** do giñee
first/last/next	**pierwszy/ostatni/ następny**	pyehrfshi/ostahtñee nahstehmpni
What time does the train from Warsaw arrive?	**O której godzinie przychodzi pociąg z Warszawy?**	o ktooray godzheeñeh pshihodzhee **potshonk** zvahrshahvi
What time does the train for Warsaw leave?	**O której godzinie odjeżdża pociąg do Warszawy?**	o ktooray godzheeñeh odyehzhjah **potshonk** do vahrshahvi
Will the train leave on time?	**Czy pociąg odejdzie punktualnie?**	chi **potshonk** odaydzheh poonktoowahlñeh
Is the train late?	**Czy pociąg jest opóźniony?**	chi **potshonk** yehst opoozynoni
Is there a dining-car on the train?	**Czy jest wagon restauracyjny?**	chi yehst **vah**gon rehstahwrahtsiyni

WEJŚCIE	ENTRANCE
WYJŚCIE	EXIT
NA PERONY	TO THE PLATFORMS

Where's the...?

Where's the...?	**Gdzie jest...?**	gdzheh yehst
bar	**bar**	bahr
buffet	**buffet**	boofeht
restaurant	**restauracja**	rehstahwrahtsyah
left luggage office	**przechowalnia bagażu**	pshehhovahlñah bahgahzhoo

lost and found office	biuro rzeczy znalezionych	byooro zhehchi znahlehzyonih
newsstand	kiosk z gazetami	kyosk zgahzehtahmee
waiting room	poczekalnia	pochehkahlñah
Where are the toilets?	Gdzie są toalety?	gdzheh sawng twahlehti

Platform (track)

What platform does the train for Cracow leave from?	Z którego peronu odchodzi pociąg do Krakowa?	sktoorehgo pehronoo othodzhee potshonk do krahkovah
What platform does the train from Warsaw arrive at?	Na który peron przychodzi pociąg z Warszawy?	nah ktoori pehron pshihodzhee potshonk zvahrshahvi
Where's platform 3?	Gdzie jest peron 3?	gdzheh yehst pehron 3
Is this the right platform for the train to...?	Czy z tego peronu odchodzi pociąg do...?	chi stehgo pehronoo othodzhee potshonk do

Possible answers

To jest pociąg bezpośredni.	It's a direct train.
Musi się pan/pani przesiąść w...	You have to change at...
W... proszę przesiąść się na pociąg podmiejski.	Change at... and get a local train.
Peron... jest...	Platform... is...
tam/w dół tymi schodami na lewo/na prawo	over there/downstairs on the left/on the right
Pociąg do... odejdzie o... z peronu...	The train to... will leave at... from platform...
Pociąg do... planowy przyjazd... będzie... minut opóźniony.	The... train for... will be... minutes late.
Pociąg z... właśnie wjeżdża na peron...	The train from... is now arriving at platform...
Ma opóźnienie... minut.	There'll be a delay of... minutes.

All aboard...

Excuse me, may I get by?	**Przepraszam, chciałbym przejść.**	pshehprahshahm htsahwbim pshaysytsh
Is this seat taken?	**Czy to miejsce jest zajęte?**	chi to myastseh yehst zahyehnteh
Is this seat free?	**Czy to miejsce jest wolne?**	chi to myaystseh yehst volneh

---

PALENIE WZBRONIONE
NO SMOKING

TRAVELLING AROUND

I think that's my seat.	**To chyba moje miejsce.**	to hibah moyeh myaystseh
Can you tell me when we get to Cracow?	**Czy może pan/ pani powiedzieć mi kiedy przyjed- ziemy do Krakowa?**	chi mozheh pahn/pahñee povyehdzhehtsh mee kehdi pshiyehdzhehmi do krahkovah
What station is this?	**Co to za stacja?**	tso to zah stahtsyah
How long does the train stop here?	**Jak długo pociąg tu stoi?**	yahk dwoogo potshonk too stoee
Can you tell me what time we get to Szczecin?	**O której godzinie przyjedziemy do Szczecina?**	o ktooray godzheeñeh pshiyehdzhehmi do shchehtsheenah

Some time on the journey the ticket-collector will come around and say: *Proszę bilety* (Tickets, please!).

Eating

Most long-distance trains have a restaurant car or a buffet car. There are no separate sittings in the restaurant car. You just go along when you feel like it. If you don't feel like moving, and you only want a beer you may be lucky enough to have a waiter come by with tea, coffee and beer.

It can be very vexing searching a long and crowded train for a restaurant car that's just been disconnected, so before you set out you may want to ask the conductor:

Is there a dining-car on this train?	**Czy w pociągu jest wagon restauracyjny?**	chi fpotshongoo yehst vahgon rehstahwrahtsiyni
In which direction is it?	**W którą stronę trzeba iść?**	fktoorawng stroneh chshehbah eesytsh
Are there any tables free?	**Czy są wolne stoliki?**	chi sawng volneh stoleekee

Sleeping

If you're on a sleeping car, your steward will have a variety of drinks, light snacks and cigarettes just down the corridor.

Are there any compartments free in the sleeping car?	**Czy są wolne miejsca w wagonie sypialnym?**	chi sawng volneh myaystsah vahgoñeh sipyahlnim
Where's the sleeping car?	**Gdzie jest wagon sypialny?**	gdzheh yehst vahgon sipyahlni
Compartments 18 and 19, please.	**Przedziały 18 i 19.**	pshehdzhahwi 18 ee 19
Would you make up our berths?	**Czy może pan/ pani przygotować nam łóżka?**	chi mozheh pahn/pahñee psigotovahtsh nahm wooshkah
Would you call me at 7 o'clock?	**Proszę mnie obudzić o 7.**	prosheh mñeh oboodzheetsh o 7
Would you bring me some coffee in the morning?	**Czy może pan/ pani przynieść mi kawę rano?**	chi mozheh pahn/pahñee pshiñehsytsh mee kahveh rahno

Timetables

If you intend to do a lot of train travel, it might be a good idea to buy a timetable. These are based on the 24-hour clock and are for sale at ticket offices, information desks and in some bookshops.

I'd like to buy a timetable.	**Proszę o rozkład jazdy.**	prosheh o roskwaht yahzdi

FOR PORTERS, see page 24

72

Bus—Tramway (streetcar)

Buses and trams provide fast and cheap transport in the cities. They almost never have a conductor. Go to a *Ruch* kiosk (there's always one nearby) and buy your ticket in advance. Buy five or ten if you're going to use the buses regularly, and when you get on the bus or tram you'll find a place to punch your ticket. If your fellow passengers don't punch tickets it's because they've a monthly pass. There are separate doors for getting on and off—use the right one: *wejście* means entrance and *wyjście* exit. If you've small children get on and off at the door nearest the driver. The same applies for trams.

Posted at bus and tram stops, you'll see information on the numbers that stop there, their routes, the times of the first and last buses and the approximate frequency of service. You'll find there are also express buses marked *pośpieszny* and night buses in cities. Express buses have letters, not numbers.

If you don't know the city very well, you may find that your map of the city has bus routes indicated on it. If you've trouble, it'll probably be best to take a taxi. They're not expensive. Don't forget: taxi fares are higher at night and beyond the city limits.

TRAVELLING AROUND

Where can I get a bus to Zakopane?	Skąd odjeżdża autobus do Zakopanego?	skont odyehzhjah ahwtoboos do zahkopahnehgo
What bus do I take for Cracow?	Jakim autobusem mogę dostać się do Krakowa?	yahkeem ahwtoboosehm mogeh dostahtsh syeh do krahkovah
Where's the...?	Gdzie jest...?	gdzheh yehst
nearest Ruch	najbliższy kiosk Ruchu	nighbleeshshi kyosk roohoo
ticket office for long-distance buses	kasa autobusów dalekobieżnych	kahsah ahwtoboosoof dahlekobyehzhnih
bus station (terminal)	dworzec autobusowy	dvozhehts ahwtoboosovi
bus stop	przystanek autobusowy	pshistahnehk ahwtoboosovi

When is the … bus to Nowy Targ?	Kiedy odjeżdża … autobus do Nowego Targu?	kehdi odyehzhjah ahwtoboos do novehgo tahrgoo
first/last/next	pierwszy/ostatni/ następny	pyehrfshi/ostahtñee/ nahstehmpni
How often do the buses to Zakopane run?	Jak często odchodzą autobusy do Zakopanego?	yahk chehnsto odhodzawng ahwtoboosi do zahkopahnehgo
Do I have to change buses?	Czy muszę się przesiadać?	chi moosheh syeh pshehsyahdahtsh
How long does the journey take?	Ile czasu trwa podróż?	eeleh chahsoo trfah podroosh
I'd like five bus tickets, please.	Proszę pięć biletów autobusowych.	prosheh pyehñtsh beelehtoof ahwtoboosovih
I'd like three tram tickets, please.	Proszę trzy bilety tramwajowe.	prosheh chshi beelehti trahmvahyoveh
How much is the fare to…?	Ile kosztuje bilet do…?	eeleh koshtooyeh beeleht do
I want a ticket to…	Proszę bilet do…	prosheh beeleht do
Will you tell me when to get off?	Czy może mi pan/ pani powiedzieć kiedy wysiąść?	chi mozheh mee pahn/ pahñee povyehdzhehtsh kehdi visyoñsytsh
I want to get off at the Palace of Culture.	Chcę wysiąść przy Pałacu Kultury.	htseh visyoñsytsh pshi pahwahtsoo kooltoori
Please let me off at the next stop.	Proszę się zatrzy- mać na następnym przystanku.	prosheh syeh zahtshi- mahtsh nah nahstehmpnim pshistahnkoo
May I have my luggage, please?	Proszę o bagaż?	prosheh o bahgahsh

Ⓣ TRAM-STOP

Ⓐ BUS-STOP

TRAVELLING AROUND

Lost!

We hope you'll have no need for the following phrases on your trip... but just in case:

Where's the lost property office?	Gdzie jest biuro rzeczy znalezionych?	gdzheh yehst **byooro zhehc** znahleh**zyo**nih
I've lost my...	Zgubiłem...	zgoo**bee**wehm
It's very valuable.	Jest bardzo wartościowa.	yehst **bahr**dzo vahrtosy**tsho**vah

Travelling and photography

At the present time there's a law in Poland which forbids photographing railway stations, bridges, military areas, harbours and airports. Feel free to use your camera as much as you want, but do remember this restriction about photographing communications.

Hitchhiking

One of the best ways to see a country is hitchhiking around it. Poland is a good country for hitchhiking. You put out an arm, not just a thumb. It is recommended that you go to one of the many tourist offices and purchase for a small sum a special hitchhiking card, which you hold out to passing drivers. It provides you with insurance against accident during your stay in Poland and there are coupons that you tear off and give your driver, giving him a bonus, too.

How far are you going?	Dokąd pan/pani jedzie?	**do**kont pahn/**pah**ñee **yeh**dzheh
Do you have room for my boy/girl friend as well?	Czy może pan zabrać mojego znajomego/moją znajomą?	chi **mo**zheh pahn **zah**brahtsh mo**yeh**go znah**yo**mehgo/mo**yawng** znah**yo**mawng
Will you drop me here, please?	Proszę mnie tu wysadzić.	**pro**sheh mñeh too vi**sah**dzheetsh
Which is the route to ...?	Gdzie jest szosa do ...?	gdzheh yehst **sho**sah do

Around and about—Sightseeing

Here we're more concerned with the cultural aspect of life than with entertainment, and, for the moment, with towns rather than the countryside. If you want a guidebook, ask...

Can you recommend a good guidebook for...?	Czy może pan/pani polecić mi dobry przewodnik po...?	chi mozheh pahn/pahñee polehtsheetsh mee dobri psehvodñeek po
Is there a tourist office here?	Czy jest tu biuro turystyczne?	chi yehst too byooro tooristichneh
Where is the tourist information centre?	Gdzie jest centralne biuro informacji turystycznej?	gdzheh yehst tsehntrahlneh byooro eenformahtsyee tooristichnay
What are the main points of interest?	Co jest najciekawsze?	tso yehst nightshehkahfsheh
We're only here for...	Będziemy tu tylko...	behñdzhehmi too tilko
a day	jeden dzień	yehdehn dzeñ
a few hours	kilka godzin	keelkah godzheen
a week	tydzień	tidzheñ
Can you recommend a sightseeing tour?	Czy może mi pan/pani polecić wycieczkę po mieście?	chi mozheh mee pahn/pahñee polehtsheetsh vitshehchkeh po myehsytsheh
Where does the bus start from?	Skąd odjeżdża autobus?	skont odyehzhjah ahwtoboos
Will it pick us up at the hotel?	Czy może nas zabrać z hotelu?	chi mozheh nahs zahbrahtsh s hotehloo
What bus/tram do we want?	Jakim autobusem/tramwajem musimy jechać?	yahkeem ahwtoboosehm/trahmvahyehm moosyeemi yehhahtsh
How much does the tour cost?	Ile kosztuje wycieczka?	eeleh koshtooyeh vitshehchkah
What time does the tour start?	O której (godzinie) zaczyna się wycieczka?	o ktooray (godzheeñeh) zahchinah syeh vitshehchkah

FOR TIME OF DAY, see page 178

We'd like to rent a car for the day.	Chcielibyśmy wynająć samochód na dzień.	hitshehleebisymi vinahyontsh sahmohoot nah dzhehñ
Is there an English-speaking guide?	Czy jest przewodnik mówiący po angielsku?	chi yehst pshehvodñeek moovyontsi po ahngehlskoo
Where is/are the...?	Gdzie jest/są...?	gdzheh yehst/sawng
antiquities	sklep z antykami	sklehp zahntikahmee
aquarium	akwarium	ahkfahryoom
art gallery	galeria sztuki	gahlehryah shtookee
botanical gardens	ogród botaniczny	ogrood botahñeechni
building	budynek	boodinehk
castle	zamek	zahmehk
cathedral	katedra	kahtehdrah
cave	jaskinia	yahskeeñah
cemetery	cmentarz	tsmehntahsh
church	kościół	kosytshoow
city walls	mury obronne	moori obronneh
concert hall	sala koncertowa	sahlah kontsehrtovah
convent	klasztor	klahshtor
docks	baseny portowe	bahsehni portoveh
downtown area	centrum	tsehntroom
exhibition	wystawa	vistahvah
factory	fabryka	fahbrikah
fortress	twierdza	tfyehrdzah
fountain	fontanna	fontahnnah
gardens	ogrody	ogrodi
glass-works	huta szkła	hootah shkwah
harbour	przystań	pshistahñ
lake	jezioro	yehzyoro
library	biblioteka	beeblotehkah
market	rynek	rinehk
memorial	pomnik	pomñeek
monastery	klasztor	klahshtor
monument	pomnik	pomñeek
museum	muzeum	moozehoom
observatory	obserwatorium	opsehrvahtoryoom
Old Town	Stare Miasto	stahreh myahsto
opera house	gmach opery	gmahh opehri
Orthodox church	cerkiew	tsehrkehf
palace	pałac	pahwahts
park	park	pahrk
Parliament building	budynek Sejmu	boodinehk saymoo
post office	poczta	pochtah

ruins	ruiny	rooeeni
shopping centre	centrum handlowe	tsehntroom hahndloveh
shrine	miejsce uświęcone	myaystseh oosyfehntsoneh
stadium	stadion	stahdyon
statue	pomnik	pomñeek
synagogue	synagoga	sinahgogah
television studios	studia telewizyjne	stoodyah tehlehveeziyneh
temple	świątynia	syfyontiñah
tomb	grób	groop
tower	wieża	vyehzhah
town centre	centrum	tsehntroom
town hall	ratusz	rahtoosh
university	uniwersytet	ooñeevehrsiteht
vaults	groby	grobi
watermill	młyn wodny	mwin vodni
windmill	wiatrak/młyn	vyahtrahk/mwin
zoo	zoo	zoo

Admission

Is the ... open on Sundays?	Czy ... jest otwarte w niedziele?	chi ... yehst otfahrteh vñehdzhehleh
When does it open?	Kiedy się otwiera?	kehdi syeh otfyehrah
When does it close?	Kiedy się zamyka?	kehdi syeh zahmikah
How much is the admission charge?	Ile kosztuje wstęp?	eeleh koshtooyeh fstehmp
Is there any reduction for ...?	Czy jest zniżka dla ...?	chi yehst zñeeshkah dlah
students/children	studentów/dzieci	stoodehntoof/dzhehtshee
Here's my ticket.	Oto mój bilet.	oto mooy beeleht
Here are our tickets.	Oto nasze bilety.	oto nahsheh beelehti
Have you a guide book (in English)?	Czy jest przewodnik (po angielsku)?	chi yehst pshehvodñeek (po ahngehlskoo)
Can I buy a catalogue?	Czy mogę kupić katalog?	chi mogeh koopeetsh kahtahlok
Is it all right to take pictures?	Czy można fotografować?	chi mozhnah fotograhfovahtsh

Who—What—When?

What's that building?	**Co to za budynek?**	tso to zah boodinehk
Who was the ...?	**Jak się nazywał...?**	yahk syeh nahzivahw
architect	**architekt**	ahrheetehkt
artist	**artysta**	ahrtistah
painter	**malarz**	mahlahsh
sculptor	**rzeźbiarz**	zhehzybyahsh
Who built it?	**Kto go zbudował?**	kto go zboodovahw
Who painted that picture?	**Kto namalował ten obraz?**	kto nahmahlovahw tehn obrahs
When did he live?	**Kiedy żył?**	kehdi zhiw
When was it built?	**Kiedy został zbudowany?**	kehdi zostahw zboodovahni
Where's the house where .... lived?	**Gdzie jest dom, w którym mieszkał...?**	gdzheh yehst dom fktoorim myehshkahw
We're interested in...	**Interesuje/ interesują nas...**	eentehrehsooyeh/ eentehrehsooyawng nahs
archaeology	**archeologia**	ahrhehologyah
art	**sztuka**	shtookah
botany	**botanika**	botahñeekah
ceramics	**ceramika**	tsehrahmeekah
coins	**monety**	monehti
fine arts	**sztuka piękna**	shtookah pyehnknah
furniture	**meble**	mehbleh
geology	**geologia**	gehologyah
history	**historia**	heestoryah
local crafts	**sztuka regionalna**	shtookah rehgyonahlnah
music	**muzyka**	moozikah
natural history	**przyro- doznawstwo**	pshirodoznahstfo
ornithology	**ornitologia**	orñeetologyah
painting	**malarstwo**	mahlahrstfo
pottery	**garncarstwo**	gahrntsahrstfo
sculpture	**rzeźba**	zhehzybah
wild life	**dzika przyroda**	dzheekah pshirodah
zoology	**zoologia**	zoologyah
Where's the ... department?	**Gdzie jest sala ...?**	gdzheh yehst sahlah

Just the adjective you've been looking for...

It's...	Jest...	yehst
amazing	zadziwiający	zahdzheevyahyontsi
awful	okropny	okropni
beautiful	piękny	pyehnkni
gloomy	ponury	ponoori
hideous	wstrętny	fstrehntni
interesting	interesujący	eentehrehsooyontsi
magnificent	wspaniały	fspahñahwi
monumental	monumentalny	monoomehntahlni
overwhelming	przytłaczający	pshitwahchahyontsi
sinister	złowrogi	zwovrogee
strange	dziwny	dzheevni
stupendous	zdumiewający	zdoomyehvahyontsi
superb	doskonały	doskonahwi
terrible	straszny	strahshni
terrifying	przerażający	pshehrahzhighyontsi
tremendous	ogromny	ogromni
ugly	brzydki	bzhitkee

SIGHTSEEING

Church services

Poland is predominantly Roman Catholic but you'll find Orthodox churches in some parts of Poland. Churches are open all the time. In cities you will find Protestant churches and synagogues. Times of services are posted in the churches. In Warsaw churches you'll find information on services in English and French in the city.

Is there a/an... near here?	Czy jest w pobliżu...?	chi yehst fpobleezhoo
Orthodox church	cerkiew	tsehrkehf
Protestant church	kościół protestancki	kosytshoow protehstahntskee
Catholic church	kościół katolicki	kosytshoow kahtoleetskee
synagogue	synagoga	sinahgogah
At what time is high mass?	O której (godzinie) jest suma?	o ktooray (godzheeñeh) yehst soomah
Where can I find a priest who speaks English?	Gdzie mogę znaleźć księdza mówiącego po angielsku?	gdzheh mohgeh znahlehsytsh ksyehndzah moovyontsehgo po ahngehlskoo

Relaxing

Cinema (movies)—Theatre

Since the cinema performances aren't continuous, you can buy
your tickets in advance. You can expect one feature film, a
newsreel, perhaps a short documentary. The time of the first
performance varies but the final one usually starts about 8 p.m.
Theatre performances start at about 7 p.m. Booking in advance
is advisable.

Poland has a lot of theatres and even if you don't follow the
Polish text, it'll be well worth your while to see a performance
at one of the more famous theatres. It's quite likely that there'll
be a play on somewhere that you already know, which you'll be
able to follow relatively well. In Wrocław there's the world
famous theatre workshop of Grotowski and the almost equally
famous puppet theatre known as the *pantomima*. And you
should definitely visit the opera house in Warsaw, housed in the
enormous *Teatr Wielki*.

For more intimate theatre there are the cellar theatres, where the
performance takes the form of a personal tête-à-tête with the
audience and where wine is served.

You can find out what's playing from newspapers and bill-
boards. In Warsaw you can buy a publication called *WIK*.

Have you a copy of WIK?	**Czy jest WIK?**	chi yehst veek
What's on at the cinema tonight?	**Co grają dziś w kinie?**	tso **grah**yawng dzheesy **fkee**ñeh
What's playing at the National Theatre?	**Co grają w Teatrze Narodowym?**	tso **grah**yawng ftehahtsheh nahro**do**vim
What sort of play is it?	**Co to jest za sztuka?**	tso to yehst zah **shtoo**kah
Who's it by?	**Kto ją napisał?**	kto yawng nah**pee**sahw

Can you recommend a…?	Czy może pan/ pani polecić mi…?	chi mozheh pahn/pahñee polehtsheetsh mee
good film	dobry film	dobri feelm
comedy	komedię	komehdyeh
something light	coś lekkiego	tsosy lehkkehgo
drama	dramat	drahmaht
musical	musical	moozikahl
revue	kabaret	kahbahreht
thriller	film sensacyjny	feelm sehnsahtsiyni
western	western	wehstehrn
At what theatre is that new play by… showing?	Gdzie grają tę nową sztukę…?	gdzeh grahyawng teh novawng shtookeh
Where's that new film by… playing?	Gdzie grają ten nowy film…?	gdzeh grahyawng tehn novi feelm
Who's in it?	Kto gra?	kto grah
Who's playing the lead?	Kto gra główną rolę?	kto grah gwoovnawng roleh
Who's the director?	Kto reżyseruje?	kto rehzhisehrooyeh
What time does it begin?	O której (godzinie) się zaczyna?	o ktooray (godzheeñeh) syeh zahchinah
What time does the show end?	O której godzinie się kończy?	o ktooray (godzheeñeh) syeh koñchi
Are there any tickets for tonight?	Czy są bilety na dzisiaj wieczór?	chi sawng beelehti nah dzheesyigh vyehchoor
I want to reserve two tickets for the show on Friday evening	Chciałbym zarezerwować dwa bilety na seans wieczorny w piątek.	htshahwbim zahrehzehrvovahtsh dvah beelehti nah sehahns vyehchorni fpyontehk
Can I have a ticket for Tuesday?	Proszę bilet na wtorek.	prosheh beeleht nah ftorehk
I want a seat in the stalls (orchestra).	Proszę miejsce na parterze.	prosheh myaystseh nah pahrtehzheh
Not too far back.	Nie za daleko z tyłu.	ñeh zah dahlehko stiwoo
Somewhere in the middle.	Gdzieś w środku.	gdzehsy fsyrotkoo

How much are the tickets?	**Ile kosztują bilety?**	eeleh koshtooyawng beelehti
May I have a programme please?	**Proszę o program.**	prosheh o prograhm
Can I check this coat?	**Czy mogę oddać płaszcz do szatni?**	chi mogeh oddahtsh pwahshch do shahtñee
Here's my ticket.	**Oto mój bilet.**	oto mooy beeleht

Possible answers

I'm sorry, we're sold out.	**Niestety wszystkie bilety wyprzedane.**
There are only a few seats in the circle (balcony) left.	**Jest jeszcze tylko kilka miejsc na balkonie.**
May I see your tickets?	**Bilety proszę.**
This is your seat.	**To pana/pani miejsce.**

It's not necessary to tip the person who shows you to your seat.

Opera—Ballet—Concert

Where's the opera house?	**Gdzie jest opera?**	gdzheh yehst opehrah
Where's the concert hall?	**Gdzie jest sala koncertowa?**	gdzheh yehst sahlah kontsehrtovah
What's on at the opera tonight?	**Co wystawiają dzisiaj w operze?**	tso vistahvyahyawng dzheesyigh vopehzheh
I'd like to see a ballet/an operetta.	**Chciałbym zobaczyć balet/operetkę.**	htshawbim zobahchitsh bahleht/opehrehtkeh
Who's singing?	**Kto śpiewa?**	kto sypyehvah
Who's dancing?	**Kto tańczy?**	kto tahñchi
What time does the programme start?	**O której (godzinie) zaczyna sie przedstawienie?**	o ktooray (godheeñeh) zahchinah syeh pshehtstahvyehñeh
What orchestra is playing?	**Jaka orkiestra gra?**	yahkah orkehstrah grah
What are they playing?	**Co grają?**	tso grahyawng
Who's the conductor?	**Kto dyryguje?**	kto dirigooyeh

RELAXING

Night clubs

Night clubs are pretty much the same the world over—particularly when it comes to inflated prices. Drinks aren't cheap, but Polish night clubs are good value for money. Most of the big hotels have a night club.

There are some reasonably priced places that provide good entertainment, so ask around. But find out the prices before you order—and allow for the various surcharges. For all night clubs a suit and tie are necessary.

Young people will find that the Interclubs that operate in summer (regular student clubs in winter) provide excellent entertainment at a very low price.

Can you recommend a good night club?	**Czy może pan/ pani polecić mi dobry klub nocny?**	chi mozheh pahn/pahñee polehtsheetsh mee dobri kloop notsni
Is there a floor show?	**Czy jest kabaret?**	gdzheh yehst kahbahreht
What time does the floor show start?	**O której (godzinie) zaczyna się kabaret?**	o ktooray (godzheeñeh) zahchinah syeh kahbahreht

And once inside...

A table for two, please.	**Proszę stolik na dwie osoby.**	prosheh stoleek nah dvyeh osobi
My name's... I reserved a table for four.	**Moje nazwisko... Zarezerwowałem stolik na cztery osoby.**	moyeh nahzveesko... zahrehzehrvovahwehm stoleek nah chtehri osobi
I telephoned you earlier.	**Dzwoniłem wcześniej.**	dzvonñeewehm fchehsyñay
We haven't got a reservation	**Nie mamy rezerwacji.**	ñeh mahmi rehzehrvahtsyee

Dancing

Where can we go dancing?	**Gdzie można pójść potańczyć?**	gdzheh mozhnah pooysytsh potahñchitsh
Is there a discotheque anywhere here?	**Czy gdzieś tu jest dyskoteka?**	chi gdzhehsy too yehst diskotehkah
There's a dance at the...	**Jest bal w...**	yehst bahl v
Would you like to dance?	**Czy mogę prosić?**	chi mogeh prosyeetsh
May I have this dance?	**Czy mogę prosić o ten taniec?**	chi mogeh prosyeetsh o tehn tahñehts

Do you happen to play...?

Chess, bridge and draughts (checkers) are popular. You may meet your match at bridge in Poland.

Do you happen to play chess?	**Czy pan/pani przypadkiem nie gra w szachy?**	chi pahn/**pah**ñee pshi**paht**kehm ñeh grah f**shah**hi
No, but I'll give you a game of draughts (checkers).	**Nie, ale możemy zagrać w warcaby.**	ñeh **ah**leh mo**zheh**mi **zah**grahtsh vvah**rtsah**bi
king	**król**	krool
queen	**królowa**	kroo**lo**vah
castle (rook)	**wieża**	**vyeh**zhah
bishop	**laufer**	**lah**wfehr
knight	**koń**	koñ
pawn	**pionek**	**pyo**nehk
Do you play cards/bridge?	**Czy pan/pani gra w karty/brydża?**	chi pahn/**pah**ñee grah f**kahr**ti/v**bri**jah
ace	**as**	ahs
king	**król**	krool
queen	**dama**	**dah**mah
jack	**walet**	**vah**leht
joker	**dżoker**	**jo**kehr
trumps	**atuty**	ah**too**ti
no trumps	**bez atu**	behs ah**too**
no bid	**pas**	pahs
double	**kontra**	**kon**trah

spades	**piki**	**pee**kee
hearts	**kiery**	**keh**ri
diamonds	**kara**	**kah**rah
clubs	**trefle**	**treh**fleh

Gambling

Take your chance in horse racing, the pools (you'll see *totolotek* advertised) or the national lottery. If you want to try your luck, the races will be your best bet. You can only stake your bet at the race course. Find out from the tourist office where the nearest race course is.

RELAXING

Sports

As far as spectator sports are concerned, soccer and boxing are certainly the most popular. But Poland offers opportunities for you to partake in great outdoor activities.

The meaning of the word Poland is "field" and the wide open spaces are yours for the taking. Mountain climbing, hiking, riding, hunting, fishing, and canoeing are among the most popular activities. For the hiker there's lots of peace, quiet and undiscovered countryside, especially in the southeast of Poland.

If you want to go on a horse-back riding holiday or to go hunting, it'd be a good idea to book this in advance.

RELAXING

Where are the tennis courts?	Gdzie są korty tenisowe?	gdzheh sawng korti tehñeesoveh
Can I hire rackets?	Czy mogę wypożyczyć rakietki?	chi mogeh vipozhichitsh rahkehtkee
What's the charge per...?	Ile kosztuje wypożyczenie na...?	eeleh koshtooyeh vipozhichehñeh nah
day	jeden dzień	yehdehn dzhehñ
round	jedną partię	yehdnawng pahrtyeh
hour	godzinę	godzheeneh
Where's the nearest race course (track)?	Gdzie jest najbliższy tor wyścigowy?	gdzheh yehst nighbleeshshi tor visytsheegovi
What's the admission charge?	Ile kosztuje wstęp?	eeleh koshtooyeh fstehmp
Is there a swimming pool here?	Czy jest tu basen?	chi yehst too bahsehn
Is it open-air or indoors?	Czy jest to basen odkryty czy zakryty?	chi yehst to bahsehn otkriti chi zahkriti
Is it heated?	Czy jest ogrzewany?	chi yehst ogzhehvahni
Can one swim in the lake?	Czy można kąpać się w jeziorze?	chi mozhnah kompahtsh syeh vyehzyozheh

I'd like to see a boxing match.	Chciałbym zobaczyć mecz bokserski.	htshahwbim zobahchitsh mehch boksehrskee
There's a lightweight fight at the... stadium tonight.	Dzisiaj na stadionie... jest mecz wagi lekkiej.	dzheesyigh nah stahdyoñeh... yehst mehch vahgee lehkkay
Can you get me a couple of tickets?	Czy może pan/pani kupić mi bilety?	chi mozheh pahn/pahñee koopeetsh mee beelehti
Is there a football match anywhere this Saturday?	Czy jest gdzieś mecz piłki nożnej w tę sobotę?	chi yehst gdzhehsy mehch peewkee nozhnay fteh soboteh
Who's playing?	Kto gra?	kto grah
Is there any good fishing around here?	Gdzie można tu pójść na ryby?	gdzheh mozhnah too pooysytsh nah ribi
Do I need a permit?	Czy muszę mieć zezwolenie?	chi moosheh myehtsh zehzvoleñeh
Where can I get one?	Gdzie je mogę dostać?	gdzheh yeh mogeh dostahtsh

RELAXING

On the beach

What's the beach like—sandy, shingle, rocky?	Jaka jest plaża—piaszczysta, kamienista, skalista?	yahkah yehst plahzhah—pyahshchistah kahmyeñeestah skahleestah
Is it safe for swimming?	Czy bezpiecznie tu pływać?	chi behspyehchñeh too pwivahtsh
Is there a lifeguard?	Czy jest ratownik?	chi yehst rahtovñeek
Is it safe for children?	Czy jest bezpiecznie dla dzieci?	chi yehst behspyehchñeh dlah dzhehtshee
The sea is very calm.	Morze jest bardzo spokojne.	mozheh yehst bahrdzo spokoyneh
There are some big waves.	Są duże fale.	sawng doozheh fahleh

RELAXING

Are there any dangerous currents?	**Czy są niebezpieczne prądy?**	chi sawng ñehbehspyehchneh prondi
What's the temperature of the water?	**Jaka jest temperatura wody?**	yahkah yehst tehmpehrahtoorah vodi
I want to hire...	**Chciałbym wypożyczyć...**	htshahwbim vipozhichitsh
an air mattress	**materac dmuchany**	mahtehrahts dmoohahni
a bathing hut	**kabinę**	kahbeeneh
a deck chair	**leżak**	lehzhahk
skin diving equipment	**sprzęt do nurkowania**	spshehnt do noorkovahñah
a sunshade	**parasol**	pahrahsol
a surfboard	**deskę wodną**	dehskeh vodnawng
a tent	**namiot**	nahmyot
some water skis	**narty wodne**	nahrti vodneh
Where can I rent...?	**Gdzie mogę wypożyczyć...?**	gdzheh mogeh vipozhichitsh
a canoe	**kajak**	kighyahk
a rowing boat	**łódź**	wootsh
a motorboat	**motorówkę**	motoroofkeh
a sailing boat	**żaglówkę**	zhahgloofkeh
What's the charge per hour?	**Ile się płaci za godzinę?**	eeleh syeh pawahtshee zah godzheeneh

---

KĄPIEL WZBRONIONA
NO BATHING

Winter sports

If you want to hike and ski and have all the necessary equipment, go ahead and enjoy yourself. The Tatra mountains are a paradise for the skier. But if you want you can take advantage of the facilities arranged by the tourist organizations. For example, it's possible to contact PTTK, *Polskie Towarzystwo Turystyczno Krajoznawcze,* and they'll arrange a hike for you and your friends, fixing up overnight stops, planning your route so that you get to somewhere you can eat about meal time.

I'd like to go to a skating rink.	**Chciałbym pojeździć na łyżwach.**	htshahwbim poyehzydzheetsh nah wizhvahh
Is there one near here?	**Czy jest gdzieś tutaj lodowisko?**	chi yehst gdzehsy tootigh lodoveesko
I want to rent some skates.	**Chciałbym wypożyczyć łyżwy.**	htshahwbim vipozhichitsh wizhvi
What are the skiing conditions like at Zakopane?	**Jakie warunki narciarskie są w Zakopanem?**	yahkeh vahroonkee nahrtshahrskeh sawng vzahkopahnehm
The snow is a little soft.	**Śnieg jest zbyt miękki.**	synehk yehst zbit myehnkee
Can I take skiing lessons there?	**Czy mogę wziąć sobie tam lekcje jazdy na nartach?**	chi mogeh vzyontsh sobyeh tahm lehktsyeh yahzdi nah nahrtahh
Is there a ski lift?	**Czy jest wyciąg?**	chi yehst vitshonk
I want to rent some skiing equipment.	**Chciałbym wypożyczyć sprzęt narciarski.**	htshahwbim vipozhichitsh spshehnt nahrtshahrskee

Camping—Countryside

If you have a car and want to see the country, take a tent.
Poland is an outdoor country and the weather is usually good
in summer but you should also be prepared for the occasional
shower. There are lots of good camping sites and wild open
country if you want to be on your own. You can obtain
a book listing camping sites and their facilities from the
tourist office and plan your itinerary to suit yourself. At the
border you can get a special camping permit which will entitle
you to camp at any Orbis camping site free of charge. It also
means that you'll not be expected to change as much money
into the local currency as the average tourist.

Camping is a popular form of holiday in Poland, and you'll
meet many friendly Poles while camping. The people of
Poland are keen to meet foreigners and there's no better place
to do it than in the informal atmosphere of the camping site.

Can we camp here?	**Czy możemy tu rozbić namioty?**	chi mozhehmi too rozbeetsh nahmyoti
Where can one camp for the night?	**Gdzie można rozbić namioty na noc?**	gdzheh mozhnah rozbeetsh nahmyoti nah nots
Is there a camping site near here?	**Czy jest gdzieś tutaj camping?**	chi yehst gdzhehsy tootigh kehmpeenk
May we camp in your field?	**Czy możemy rozbić namioty na pana/pani polu?**	chi mozhehmi rozbeetsh nahmyoti nah pahnah/pahñee poloo
Can we park our caravan (trailer) here?	**Czy można tu zaparkować przyczepę?**	chi mozhnah too zahpahrkovahtsh pshichehpeh
Is this an official camping site?	**Czy to jest zorganizowany camping?**	chi to yehst zorgahñeezovahni kehmpeenk
May we light a fire?	**Czy możemy rozpalić ognisko?**	chi mozhehmi rospahleetsh ogñeesko

FOR CAMPING EQUIPMENT, see page 106

s there drinking vater?	**Czy jest woda do picia?**	chi yehst **vo**dah do **peet**shah
Vhat are the acilities?	**Jakie jest wyposażenie campingu?**	**yah**keh yehst viposah**zheh**ñeh kehm**peen**goo
are there shopping acilities on the site?	**Czy na miejscu są sklepy?**	chi nah **myays**tsoo sawng **skleh**pi
are there...?	**Czy są...?**	chi sawng
aths	**łazienki**	wah**zyehn**kee
howers	**prysznice**	prish**ñeet**seh
oilets	**toalety**	twah**leh**ti
Vhat's the harge...?	**Ile kosztuje...?**	**ee**leh kosh**too**yeh
er day	**dziennie**	**dzheh**ñ̃eh
er person	**od osoby**	ot o**so**bi
or a car	**za samochód**	zah sah**mo**hoot
or a tent	**za namiot**	zah **nahm**yot
or a caravan	**za przyczepę**	zah pshi**cheh**peh
s there a youth hostel anywhere ear here?	**Czy jest gdzieś tutaj schronisko?**	chi yehst gdzhehsy **too**tigh shro**ñees**ko
o you know anyone vho can put us up or the night?	**Gdzie możemy przenocować?**	gdzheh mo**zheh**mi pshehno**tso**vahtsh

---

CAMPING WZBRONIONY
CAMPING PROHIBITED

---

low far is it to...?	**Jak daleko jest do...?**	yahk dah**leh**ko yehst do
low far is the next illage?	**Jak daleko jest do następnej wioski?**	yahk dah**leh**ko yehst do nahs**tehm**pnay **vyos**kee
are we on the right oad for...?	**Czy to jest droga do...?**	chi to yehst **dro**gah do
Vhere does this road ead to?	**Dokąd prowadzi ta droga?**	**do**kont pro**vah**dzhee tah **dro**gah
s there a scenic oute to...?	**Czy jest ładny szlak do...?**	chi yehst **wahd**ni shlahk do

Landmarks

bridge	**most**	most
brook	**potok**	po**tok**
building	**budynek**	**boodi**nehk
canal	**kanał**	**kah**nahw
church	**kościół**	**kosy**tshoow
cliff	**skała**	**skah**wah
cottage	**chata**	**hah**tah
farm	**gospodarstwo**	gospo**dahr**stfo
ferry	**prom**	prom
field	**pole**	**pol**eh
footpath	**ścieżka**	**sytshehsh**kah
forest	**las**	lahs
hamlet	**wioska**	**vyos**kah
heath	**wrzosowisko**	vzhoso**vees**ko
hill	**wzgórze**	vz**gooz**heh
house	**dom**	dom
inn	**gospoda**	gos**pod**ah
lake	**jezioro**	yeh**zyor**o
marsh	**bagno**	**bah**gno
mountain	**góra**	**goor**ah
mountain range	**łańcuch górski**	**wahñtsooh goor**skee
path	**ścieżka**	**sytshehsh**kah
peak	**wierzchołek**	vyehsh**how**ehk
pool	**sadzawka**	sah**dzahf**kah
river	**rzeka**	**zhehk**ah
road	**droga**	**drog**ah
spring	**źródło**	**zyrood**wo
stream	**strumień**	**stroom**yehñ
track	**koleina**	kole**heen**ah
tree	**drzewo**	**jzheh**vo
valley	**dolina**	do**leen**ah
village	**wieś**	vyehsy
waterfall	**wodospad**	vodo**spaht**
wood	**las**	lahs

Making friends

This shouldn't be difficult as Poles are very friendly and always interested in meeting foreigners.

Introductions

How do you do?	Dzień dobry.	dzhehñ dobri
How are you?	Jak się pan/pani ma?	yahk syeh pahn/pahñee mah
Very well, thank you.	Dobrze, dziękuję.	dobzheh dzhehnkooyeh
Fine, thanks. And you?	Dobrze. A pan/pani?	dobzheh. ah pahn/pahñee
May I introduce Miss Philips?	To jest pani Philips.	to yehst pahñee Philips
I'd like you to meet a friend of mine.	Chciałbym, aby pan poznał mojego przyjaciela.	htshahwbim ahbi pahn poznahw moyehgo pshiyahtshehlah
John, this is...	John, to pan/pani...	john to pahn/pahñee
My name's...	Nazywam się...	nahzivahm syeh
Glad to know you.	Miło mi.	meewo mee

Follow-up

How long have you been here?	Od jak dawna pan/pani jest tutaj?	ot yahg dahvnah pahn/pahñee yehst tootigh
Is this your first visit?	Czy jest pan/pani tu po raz pierwszy?	chi yehst pahn/pahñee too po rahs pyehrfshi
Are you on your own?	Czy pan/pani jest tu sam/sama?	chi pahn/pahñee yehst too sahm/sahmah
I'm with...	Jestem z...	yehstehm z
my wife	żoną	zhonawng
my family	rodziną	rodzheenawng
my parents	rodzicami	rodzheetsahmee
some friends	przyjaciółmi	psiyahtshoowmee

Are you enjoying your stay?	Czy panu/pani się tu podoba?	chi pahnoo/pahñee syeh too podobah
Where do you come from?	Skąd pan/pani pochodzi?	skont pahn/pahñee pohodzhee
What part of... do you come from?	Z której części... pan/pani pochodzi?	sktooray chehñsytshee... pahn/pahñee pohodzhee
I'm from...	Pochodzę z...	pohodzheh z
I'm a student.	Jestem studentem/studentką.	yehstehm stoodehntehm/stoodehntkawng
We're here on holiday.	Jesteśmy tu na urlopie.	yehstehsymi too nah oorlopyeh
I'm here on a business trip.	Jestem tu służbowo.	yehstehm too swoozhbovo
What kind of business are you in?	Gdzie pan pracuje?	gdzheh pahn prahtsooyeh
See you later/See you tomorrow.	Na razie/Do jutra.	nah rahzyeh/do yootrah
I'm sure we'll run into each other again some time.	Na pewno się jeszcze spotkamy.	nahpehvno syeh yehshcheh spotkahmi

The weather

Always a good topic for conversation in Poland as elsewhere.

What a lovely day!	Jaki piękny dzień!	yahkee pyehnkni dzhehñ
What awful weather.	Jaka okropna pogoda.	yahkah okropnah pogodah
Isn't it hot today?	Gorąco dzisiaj, prawda?	gorontso dzheesyigh prahvdah
Is it usually as warm as this?	Czy zawsze jest tak ciepło?	chi zahvsheh yehst tahk tshehpwo
What's the temperature outside?	Jaka jest temperatura na dworze?	yahkah yehst tehmpehrahtoorah nah dvozheh
The wind is very strong.	Jest silny wiatr.	yehst syeelni vyahtr

Invitations

My wife and I would like you to have dinner with us on…	Chcielibyśmy zaprosić pana/panią na kolację w…	htshehleebisymi zahprosyeetsh pahnah/pahñawng nah kolahtsyeh v
Can you come to dinner tomorrow night?	Czy może pan/pani przyjść na kolację jutro wieczorem?	chi mozheh pahn/pahñee pshiysytsh nah kolahtsyeh yootro vyehchorehm
We're giving a small party tomorrow night. I do hope you can come.	Urządzamy małe przyjęcie jutro wieczorem. Mam nadzieję, że pan/pani może przyjść.	oozhondzahmi mahweh pshiyehñtsheh yootro vyehchorehm. mahm nahdzhehyeh zheh pahn/pahñee mozhee pshiysytsh
Can you come round for a drink this evening?	Czy mógłby pan/pani wpaść na drinka dziś wieczorem?	chi moogbi pahn/pahñee fpahsytsh nah dreenkah dzheesy vyehchorehm
There's a party. Are you coming?	Urządzamy przyjęcie. Czy pan/pani przyjdzie.	oozhondzahmi pshiyehñtsheh chi pahn/pahñee pshiydzheh
That's very kind of you.	Dziękuję. Z przyjemnością.	dzhehnkooyeh. spshiyehmnosytshawng
Great. I'd love to come.	Cudownie. Bardzo chciałbym/chciałabym przyjść.	tsoodovñeh. bahrdzo htshahwbim/htshahwahbim pshiysytsh
What time shall we come?	O której (godzinie) mamy przyjść?	o ktooray (godzheeñeh) mahmi pshiysytsh
May I bring a friend?	Czy mogę kogoś przyprowadzić?	chi mogeh kogosy pshiprovahdzheetsh
I'm afraid we've got to go now.	Niestety musimy już iść.	ñehstehti moosyeemi yoosh eesytsh
Next time you must come to visit us.	Następnym razem prosimy do nas.	nahstehmpnim rahzehm prosyeemi do nahs
Thank you very much for an enjoyable evening	Dziękujemy za miły wieczór.	dzhehnkooyehmi zah meewi vyehchoor

MAKING FRIENDS

Dating

Would you like a cigarette?	Czy zapali pani?	chi zahpahlee pahñee
Have you got a light, please?	Czy mogę prosić o ogień?	chi mogeh prosyeetsh o ogehñ
Can I get you a drink?	Czy nie zechciałaby pani napić się czegoś?	chi ñeh zehhtshahwahbi pahñee nahpeetsh syeh chehgosy
I'm lost. Can you show me the way to...?	Zgubiłem się. Czy może pan/ pani pokazać mi drogę do...?	zgoobeewehm syeh. chi mozheh pahn/pahñee pokahzahtsh mee drogeh do
Are you free this evening?	Czy pan/pani ma dzisiaj wolny wieczór?	chi pahn/pahñee mah dzheesyigh volni vyehchoor
Would you like to go dancing?	Czy chciałaby pani pójść potańczyć?	chi htshahwahbi pahñee pooysytsh potahñchitsh
Shall we go to the cinema (movies)?	Może poszlibyśmy do kina?	mozheh poshleebisymi do keenah
Would you like to go for a drive?	Czy nie ma pani ochoty na przejażdżkę?	chi ñeh mah pahñee ohoti nah pshehyahshchkeh
Where shall we meet?	Gdzie się spotkamy?	gdzheh syeh spotkahmi
I'll pick you up at your hotel.	Przyjadę po panią do hotelu.	pshiyahdeh po pahñawng do hotehloo
I'll call for you at eight.	Wpadnę o ósmej.	fpahdneh o oosmay
May I take you home?	Czy mogę panią odwieźć do domu?	chi mogeh pahñawng odvyehsytsh do domoo
Thank you, it's been a wonderful evening.	Dziękuję za cudowny wieczór.	dzhehnkooyeh zah tsoodovni vyehchoor
What's your telephone number?	Jaki jest pana/ pani telefon?	yahkee yehst pahnah/pahñee tehlehfon
What time is your last train?	O której ma pan/ pani ostatni pociąg?	o ktooray mah pahn/pahñee ostahtñee potshonk

Shopping guide

This shopping guide is designed to help you find what you want with ease, accuracy and speed. It features:

1. a list of the different kinds of shops, stores and services;

2. some general expressions required when shopping to allow you to be specific and selective;

3. full details of the shops and services most likely to concern you. Here you'll find advice, alphabetical lists of items and conversion charts listed under headings below.

	Main items	Page
Bookshop	books, stationery	104
Camping	camping equipment	106
Chemist's (pharmacy)	medicine, first-aid, cosmetics, toilet articles	108
Clothing	clothes, shoes, accessories	112
Electrical appliances	radios, tape recorders, etc., records	119
Hairdresser's	barber's, ladies' hairdresser's, beauty salon	121
Jeweller's	jewellery, watches, watch repairs	123
Kiosk	newspapers and cigarettes	126
Laundry—Dry cleaning	usual facilities	128
Photography	cameras, accessories, films, developing	129
Provisions	this is confined to basic items required for picnics	131
Souvenirs	souvenirs, gifts, fancy goods	133

Shops, stores and services

In Poland shops are open from 9 or 10 a.m. till 7 or 8 p.m., Monday to Saturday. As the opening hours differ from place to place it's best to check in advance.

Visitors from Western countries should take advantage of the *Pewex* stores found in all big cities (very often there'll also be a shop in your hotel); these shops only accept foreign currency. They offer Polish and foreign drinks and a wide variety of Western goods (including cigarettes).

Cepelia shops specialize in handicraft and folkloric articles; credit cards, hard currency and złotys are accepted. A chain of *Desa* shops sells works of art.

A delivery service isn't normally available from the kinds of shops at which you'll be making purchases.

Where's the nearest...?	Gdzie jest najbliższy/ najbliższa...?	gdzheh yehst nighbleeshshi/ nighbleeshshah
antique shop	sklep z antykami	sklehp zahntikahmee
art gallery	sklep z obrazami	sklehp zobrahzahmee
baker's	piekarnia	pyehkahrñah
bank	bank	bahnk
barber's	fryzjer męski	friz-yehr mehnskee
beauty parlour	gabinet kosmetyczny	gahbeeneht kosmehtichni
bookshop	księgarnia	ksyehngahrñah
bookstore	stoisko z książkami	stoeesko sksyonshkahmee
butcher's	sklep mięsny	sklehp myehnsni
cable office	poczta	pochtah
camera store	fotooptyka	fotooptikah
chemist's	apteka	ahptehkah
confectioner's	cukiernia	tsookehrñah
dairy shop	mleczarnia	mlehchahrñah
delicatessen	delikatesy	dehleekahtehsi
dentist	dentysta	dehntistah
department store	dom towarowy	dom tovahrovi
doctor	lekarz	lehkahsh
draper's (dry goods store)	sklep tekstylny	sklehp tehkstilni
dressmaker's	zakład krawiecki	zahkwaht krahvyehtskee

drugstore	apteka	ahptehkah
filling station	stacja benzynowa	stahtsyah behnzinovah
fishmonger's	sklep rybny	sklehp ribni
florist's	kwiaciarnia	kfyahtshahrñah
furrier's	sklep z futrami	sklehp sfootrahmee
garage	warsztat samochodowy	vahrshtaht sahmohodovi
greengrocer's	sklep warzywniczy	sklehp vahzhivñeechi
grocery	sklep spożywczy	sklehp spozhivchi
hairdresser (ladies)	fryzjer (damski)	friz-yehr (dahmskee)
hospital	szpital	shpeetahl
jeweller's	jubiler	yoobeelehr
kiosk	kiosk Ruchu	kyosk roohoo
laundry	pralnia	prahlñah
liquor store	sklep monopolowy	sklehp monopolovi
market	targ	tahrk
milliner's	pasmanteria	pahsmahntehryah
news-stand	kiosk Ruchu	kyosk roohoo
optician	sklep optyczny	sklehp optichni
pharmacy	apteka	ahptehkah
photo shop	fotooptyka	fotooptikah
post office	poczta	pochtah
shoemaker (repairs)	szewc	shehfts
shoe shop	sklep obuwniczy	sklehp oboovñeechi
souvenir shop	sklep z pamiątkami	sklehp spahmyontkahmee
sporting goods shop	sklep sportowy	sklehp sportovi
stationer's	sklep papierniczy (Ruch)	sklehp pahpyehrñeechi (rooh)
supermarket	Sam	sahm
tailor's	krawiec	krahvyehts
tobacconist's	kiosk Ruchu	kyosk roohoo
toy shop	sklep z zabawkami	sklehp zzahbahfkahmee
travel agent	biuro podróży	byooro podroozhi
veterinarian	lecznica weterynaryjna	lehchñeetsah vehtehrinahriynah
watch maker's	zegarmistrz	zehgahrmeeshch

SHOPPING GUIDE

REMANENT CLOSED FOR INVENTORY
REMONT CLOSED FOR RENOVATION

General expressions

Here are some expressions which will be useful to you when you're out shopping.

Where?

Where's a good...?	**Gdzie jest dobry...?**	gdzheh yehst **dobri**
Where's the nearest...?	**Gdzie jest najbliższy...?**	gdzheh yehst nigh**bleesh**shi
Where can I find a...?	**Gdzie mogę znaleźć...?**	gdzheh **mogeh** **znah**lehsytsh
Can you recommend an inexpensive...?	**Czy może pan/pani polecić mi niedrogi...?**	chi **mozheh** pahn/**pah**ñee poleht**sheetsh** mee ñeh**drogee**
Where's the main shopping centre?	**Gdzie jest centrum handlowe?**	gdzheh yehst **tsehn**troom hahnd**lo**veh
How do I get there?	**Jak tam się mogę dostać?**	yahk tahm syeh **mogeh** **do**stahtsh

Service

Can you help me?	**Proszę pana/panią!**	**pro**sheh **pah**nah/**pah**ñawng
I'm just looking around.	**Chcę się tylko rozejrzeć.**	htseh syeh **til**ko rozay**zheh**tsh
I want...	**Proszę...**	**pro**sheh
Can you show me some...?	**Czy może mi pan/pani pokazać...**	chi **mozheh** mee pahn/**pah**ñee poka**zah**tsh
Have you any...?	**Czy jest/są...?**	chi yehst/sawng

That one

Can you show me...?	**Czy pan/pani może pokazać mi...?**	chi pahn/**pah**ñee **mozheh** poka**zah**tsh mee
that/those	**ten/te**	tehn/teh
the one in the window	**to z wystawy**	to zvi**stah**vi
It's over there.	**Jest tam.**	yehst tahm

Defining the article

I'd like a... one.	Chciałbym ten...	htshahwbim tehn
big	duży	doozhi
cheap	tani	tahñee
dark	ciemny	tshehmni
good	dobry	dobri
heavy	ciężki	tshehnshke
large	duży	doozhi
light (weight)	lekki	lehkkeé
light (colour)	jasny	yahsni
oval	owalny	ovahlni
rectangular	prostokątny	prostokontni
round	okrągły	okrongwi
small	mały	mahwi
square	kwadratowy	kfahdrahtovi
I don't want anything too expensive.	Nie chcę nic drogiego.	ñeh htseh ñeets drogehgo

Preference

I prefer something of better quality.	Wolę coś lepszej jakości.	voleh tsosy lehpshay yahkosytshee
Can you show me some more?	Czy może mi pan/ pani pokazać trochę więcej?	chi mozheh mee pahn/ pahñee pokahzahtsh troheh vyehntsay
Haven't you anything...?	Czy jest coś...?	chi yehst tsosy
cheaper/better	tańszego/ lepszego	tahñshehgo/ lehpshehgo
larger/smaller	większego/ mniejszego	vyehnkshehgo/ mñayshehgo

How much?

How much is this?	Ile to kosztuje?	eeleh to koshtooyeh
How much are they?	Ile one kosztują?	eeleh oneh koshtooyawng
I don't understand. Please write it down.	Nie rozumiem. Proszę napisać.	ñeh rozoomyehm. prosheh nahpeesahtsh
I don't want to spend more than ... złotys.	Nie chcę wydać więcej niż ... złotych.	ñeh htseh vidahtsh vyehntsay ñeesh... zwotih

Decision

That's just what I want.	**Właśnie to chcę.**	vwahsyñeh to htseh
It's not quite what I want.	**Nie to chciałem.**	ñeh to **htshah**wehm
Can this be taken out of the country?	**Czy można to wywieźć za granicę?**	chi **mozh**nah to vivyehtsytsh zah grah**ñee**tseh
Will I have any difficulty with the customs?	**Czy będę miał/ miała trudności z cłem?**	chi **behn**deh myahw/ myahwah trood**nosy**tshee stswehm
I'll take it.	**Wezmę to.**	**vehz**meh to

Ordering

Can you order it for me?	**Czy może pan/ pani to dla mnie zamówić?**	chi **mozh**eh pahn/**pah**ñee to dlah mñeh zah**moo**veetsh
How long will it take?	**Ile to będzie trwało?**	**ee**leh to **behñ**dzheh **tr**fahwo
I'd like it as soon as possible.	**Chciałbym to mieć jak najszybciej.**	**htshahw**bim to myehtsh yahk nigh**ship**tshay

Paying

How much is it?	**Ile to kosztuje?**	**ee**leh to **kosh**tooyeh
Can I pay by traveller's cheque (check)?	**Czy mogę zapłacić czekami pdróżnymi?**	chi **mo**geh zah**pwah**tsheetsh cheh**kah**mee podroozh**hni**mee
Do you accept credit cards?	**Czy przyjmuje się karty kredytowe?**	chi pshiy**moo**yeh syeh **kah**rti krehdi**to**veh
Haven't you made a mistake in the bill?	**Czy pani nie pomyliła się w rachunku?**	chi **pah**ñee ñeh pomi**lee**wah syeh vrah**hoon**koo
Can I have a receipt, please?	**Proszę o paragon.**	**pro**sheh o pah**rah**gon
Will you wrap it, please?	**Proszę to zapakować.**	**pro**sheh to zahpah**ko**vahtsh

Anything else?

No, thanks, that's all.	**Dziękuję to wszystko.**	dzhehn**kooy**eh to **fshis**tko
Let me see—I want...	**Chwileczkę. Chciałbym...**	hfee**lehch**keh: htsha**hw**bim
Show me...	**Proszę mi pokazać...**	**pro**sheh mee po**kah**zahtsh
Thank you. Good-bye.	**Dziękuję. Do widzenia.**	dzh**hehn**kooyeh. do veedzeh**ñah**

Dissatisfied

I want to return this.	**Chciałbym/ chciałabym to zwrócić.**	htsha**hw**bim/ htsha**hw**ahbim to zvroot**sheetsh**
I'd like a refund. Here's the receipt.	**Proszę o zwrot pieniędzy. Oto paragon.**	**pro**sheh o zvrot pyeh**ñehn**dzi. oto pah**rah**gon

---

Possible answers

Słucham?	Can I help you?
Jaki... chce pan/pani?	What... would you like?
kolor/kształt	colour/shape
Jakiej jakości chce pan/pani?	What quality would you like?
Ile pan/pani chce?	How many?
Niestety nie ma. Wszystko sprzedane.	I'm sorry, we haven't any. We're out of stock.
Czy mamy to dla pana/ pani zamówić?	Shall we order it for you?
... złotych proszę.	That's ... złotys, please.
Nie przyjmujemy...	We don't accept...
kart kredytowych czeków podróżnych czeków	credit cards traveller's cheques personal cheques

Bookshop—Stationer's

In Poland bookshops and stationer's are usually separate shops.
Newspapers and magazines are sold at *Ruch* kiosks.

Where's the nearest...?	Gdzie jest w pobliżu...?	gdzheh yehst fpobleezhoo
bookshop	księgarnia	ksyehngahrñah
stationer's	sklep papierniczy (Ruch)	sklehp pahpyehrñeechi (rooh)
Can you recommend a good bookshop?	Czy może pan/ pani polecić mi dobrą księgarnię?	chi mozheh pahn/pahñee polehtsheetsh mee dobrawng ksyehngahrñeh
I want to buy a/an/some...	Proszę...	prosheh
address book	notatnik alfabetyczny	notahtñeek ahlfahbehtichni
ball-point pen	długopis	dwoogopees
book	książkę	ksyonshkeh
box of paints	pudełko farb	poodehwko fahrp
carbon paper	kalkę	kahlkeh
cellotape	taśmę samoprzylepną	tahsymeh sahmopzhilehpnawng
crayons	kredki	krehtkee
dictionary	słownik	swovñeek
Polish-English	polsko-angielski	polsko-ahngehlskee
English-Polish	angielsko-polski	ahngehlsko-polskee
pocket	kieszonkowy	kehshonkovi
drawing paper	karton rysunkowy	kahrton risoonkovi
drawing pins	pineski	peeneskee
envelopes	koperty	kopehrti
eraser	gumkę	goomkeh
file	klasyfikator	klahsifeekahtor
fountain pen	pióro wieczne	pyooro vyehchneh
glue	klej	klay
grammar book	gramatykę	grahmahtikeh
guide book	przewodnik	pshehvodñeek
ink	atrament	ahtrahmehnt
black/red/blue	czarny/czer- wony/niebieski	chahrni/chehrvoni/ ñehbyehskee
labels	naklejki	nahklaykee
map	mapę	mahpeh
map of the town	plan miasta	plahn myahstah
road map	mapę drogową	mahpeh drogovawng
notebook	notatnik	notahtñeek

note paper	wkład do notatnika	fkwand do notaht**ñee**kah
paperback	książkę	ksyonshkeh
paper napkins	serwetki papierowe	sehr**veht**kee pahpyeh**ro**veh
paste	biały klej	byah**wi** klay
pen	pióro	pyooro
pencil	ołówek	o**woo**vehk
pencil sharpener	temperówkę	tehmpeh**roof**keh
refill (for a pen)	wkład (do długopisu)	fkwahd (do dwoogo**pee**soo)
rubber bands	gumkę do związywania	**goom**keh do zvyonzi**vah**ñah
ruler	linijkę	lee**ñee**eykeh
Scotch tape	taśmę samoprzylepną	**tah**symeh sahmopzhi**lehp**nawng
sketching block	blok rysunkowy	blok risoon**kovi**
string	sznurek	**shnoo**rehk
thumbtacks	pineski	pee**nehs**kee
tissue paper	bibułkę	bee**boow**keh
tracing paper	pergamin	pehr**gah**meen
typewriter ribbon	taśmę do maszyny	**tah**symeh do mah**shi**ni
typing paper	papier maszynowy	**pah**pyehr mah**shi**novi
wrapping paper	papier do pakowania	**pah**pyehr do pahko**vah**ñah
writing pad	papeterię (blok listowy)	pahpeh**teh**ryeh (blok **lees**tovi)
Where's the guide-book section?	Gdzie są przewodniki turystyczne?	gdzheh sawng psehvod**ñee**kee tooris**tich**neh
Where do you keep the English books?	Gdzie są książki angielskie?	gdyeh sawng **ksyon**shkee ahn**gehl**skeh
Have you any of...'s books in English?	Czy ma pan/pani jakieś angielskie tłumaczenie...?	chi mah pahn/**pah**ñee **yah**kehsy ahn**gehl**skeh twoomah**cheh**ñeh
Is there an English translation of...?	Czy jest angielskie tłumaczenie...?	chi yehst ahn**gehl**skeh twoomah**cheh**ñeh

SHOPPING GUIDE

Camping

Here we're concerned with the equipment you may need.

I'd like a/an/some...	Proszę...	prosheh
axe	siekierkę	syehkehrkeh
bottle opener	otwieracz butelek	otfyehrahch bootehlehk
bucket	wiadro	vyahdro
butane gas	gaz w butli	gahz vbootlee
camp bed	składane łóżko	skwahdahneh wooshko
camping equipment	sprzęt campingowy	spshehnt kehmpeengovi
can opener	klucz do konserw	klooch do konsehrf
candles	świece	syfyehtseh
chair	krzesło	kshehswo
folding chair	składane krzesło	skwahdahneh kshehswo
compass	kompas	kompahs
corkscrew	korkociąg	korkotshonk
crockery	naczynia stołowe	nahchiñah stowoveh
cutlery	sztućce	shtootshtseh
deck chair	leżak	lehzhahk
first-aid kit	apteczkę podręczną	ahptehchkeh podrehnchnawng
fishing tackle	sprzęt wędkarski	spshehnd vehntkahrskee
flashlight	latarkę	lahtahrkeh
frying pan	patelnię	pahtelñeh
groundsheet	podłogę namiotową	podwogeh nahmyotovawng
hammer	młotek	mwotehk
hammock	hamak	hahmahk
ice bag	lodówkę turystyczną	lodoofkeh tooristichnawng
kerosene	naftę	nahfteh
kettle	czajnik	chighñeek
knapsack	plecak	plehtsahk
lamp	lampę	lahmpeh
lantern	lampę	lahmpeh
matches	zapałki	zahpahwkee
mattress	materac	mahtehrahts
methylated spirits	spirytus metylowy	speeritoos mehtilovi
mosquito net	moskitierę	moskeetyehreh
pail	wiadro	vyahdro
paraffin	naftę	nahfteh
penknife	scyzoryk	stsizorik
picnic case	koszyk	koshik
rope	linkę	leenkeh

rucksack	plecak	plehtsahk
saucepan	rondel	rondehl
scissors	nożyczki	nozhichkee
screwdriver	śrubokręt	syroobokrehnt
sheath knife	finkę	feenkeh
sleeping bag	śpiwór	sypeevoor
stewpan	patelnię	pahtehlñeh
stove	kuchenkę gazową	koohehnkeh gahzovawng
table	stolik	stoleek
folding table	stolik składany	stoleek skwahdahni
tent	namiot	nahmyot
tent peg	śledź	sylehtsh
tent pole	maszt	mahsht
thermos flask (bottle)	termos	tehrmos
tin opener	klucz do konserw	klooch do konsehrf
tongs	obcążki	optsonshkee
tool kit	zestaw narzędzi	zehstahf nahzhehndzhee
torch	latarkę	lahtahrkeh
vacuum flask	termos	tehrmos
water carrier	pojemnik na wodę	poyehmñeek nah vodeh
wood alcohol	spirytus metylowy	speeritoos mehtilovi

Crockery

beakers	kubki plastikowe	koopkee plahsteekoveh
cups	filiżanki	feeleezhahnkee
food box	pojemnik na żywność	poyehmñeek nah zhivnosytsh
mugs	kubki	koopkee
plates	talerze	tahlehzheh
saucers	spodki	spotkee

Cutlery

forks	widelce	veedehltseh
knives	noże	nozheh
dessert knife	nożyk	nozhik
spoons	łyżki	wishkee
tea-spoons	łyżeczki	wizhehchkee
made of plastic	z plastiku	splahsteekoo
made of stainless steel	ze stali nierdzewnej	zeh stahlee ñehrdzehvnay

Chemist's (pharmacy)—Drugstore

An *apteka* is a place where you buy all your medical require
ments and a *drogeria* is a place where you buy your toilet and
cosmetic requirements. Sometimes you will see a *perfumeria*
which specialises in cosmetics. Look out for the special *Pollena*
cosmetics shops.

There's a round-the-clock service at the *apteka*. Look on the
door of your closest *apteka* and you'll see a notice giving the
address of the nearest one that's open.

This section is divided into two parts:

1. Pharmaceutical—medicine, first-aid, etc.
2. Toiletry—toilet articles, cosmetics

Where's the nearest (all night) chemist?	**Gdzie jest najbliższa apteka (na dyżurze nocnym)?**	gdzheh yehst nigh-bleeshshah ahptehkah (nah dizhoozheh notsnim)
What time does the chemist open/close?	**O której (godzinie) otwiera/zamyka się apteka?**	o ktooray (godzheeñeh) otfyehrah/zahmikah syeh ahptehkah

Part 1—Pharmaceutical

I want something for...	**Proszę coś na...**	prosheh tsosy nah
a cold	**przeziębienie**	pshehzyehmbyehñeh
a cough	**kaszel**	kahshehl
hay fever	**katar sienny**	kahtahr syehnni
a hangover	**kaca**	kahtsah
sunburn	**oparzenie słoneczne**	opahzhehñeh swonehchneh
travel sickness	**mdłości**	mdwosytshee
Can you make up this prescription?	**Czy może pani zrobić to lekarstwo?**	chi mozheh pahñee zrobeetsh to lehkahrstfo
When shall I come back?	**Kiedy mam przyjść?**	kehdi mahm pshiysytsh

FOR DOCTOR, see page 162

Can I get it without prescription?	**Czy mogę to dostać bez recepty?**	chi mogeh to dostahtsh behs rehtsehpti
Can I have a/an/some...?	**Proszę...**	prosheh
antiseptic cream	**krem antyseptyczny**	krehm ahntisehptichni
bandage	**bandaż**	bahndahsh
crepe bandage	**bandaż elastyczny**	bahndahsh ehlahstichni
gauze bandage	**bandaż gazowy**	bahndahsh gahzovi
band-aids	**plaster**	plahstehr
calcium tablets	**wapno w tabletkach**	vahpno ftahblehtkahh
contraceptives	**prezerwatywy**	prehzehrvahtivi
corn plasters	**plaster na odciski**	plahstehr nah ottsheeskee
cotton wool	**watę**	vahteh
cough lozenges	**tabletki na kaszel**	tahblehtkee nah kahshehl
diabetic lozenges	**tabletki na cukrzycę**	tahblehtkee nah tsookshitseh
disinfectant	**środek dezynfekujący**	syrodehk dehzinfehkooyontsi
ear drops	**krople do uszu**	kropleh do ooshoo
elastoplast	**plaster**	plahstehr
eye drops	**krople do oczu**	kropleh do ochoo
gargle	**płyn do płukania gardła**	pwin do pwookahñah gahrdwah
gauze	**gazę opatrunkową**	gahzeh opahtroonkovawng
insect repellent	**płyn przeciw owadom**	pwin pshehtsheef ovahdom
iodine	**jodynę**	yodineh
iron pills	**tabletki żelaza**	tahblehtkee zhehlahzah
laxative	**środek na przeczyszczenie**	syrodehk nah pshehchishchehñeh
lint	**gazę**	gahzeh
mouthwash	**płyn do ust**	pwin do oost
sanitary napkins	**opaskę higieniczną**	opahskeh heegehñeechnawng
sleeping pills	**środek nasenny**	syrodehk nahsehnni
stomach pills	**tabletki na żołądek**	tahblehtkee nah zhowondehk
throat lozenges	**tabletki na gardło**	tahblehtkee nah gahrdwo
tissues	**ligninę**	leegñeeneh
tranquillizers	**środki uspokajające**	syrotkee oospokahyahyontseh
vitamin pills	**witaminy**	veetahmeeni

SHOPPING GUIDE

Part 2—Toiletry

I'd like a/an/some...	Proszę...	prosheh
acne cream	krem na skórę	krehm nah skooreh
after-shave lotion	płyn po goleniu	pwin po golehñoo
astringent	środek wstrzymujący	syrodehk fstshimooyontsi
bath cubes	szyszki kąpielowe	shishkee kompyehloveh
bath salts	sole kąpielowe	soleh kompyehloveh
cream	krem	krehm
cleansing cream	mleczko kosmetyczne	mlehchko kosmehtichneh
foundation cream	podkład	potkwaht
hormone cream	krem hormonalny	krehm hormonahlni
moisturizing cream	krem nawilżający	krehm nahveelzhahyontsi
night cream	krem na noc	krehm nah nots
cuticle remover	cążki	tsonshkee
deodorant	dezodorant	dehzodorahnt
eau de Cologne	wodę kolońską	vodeh kolońskawng
eye liner	tusz do rzęs	toosh do zhehns
eye pencil	ołówek do powiek	owoovehk do povyehk
eye shadow	cień do powiek	tshehñ do povyehk
face pack	maseczkę kosmetyczną	mahsehchkeh kosmehtichnawng
face powder	puder	poodehr
foot cream	krem do stóp	krehm do stoop
hand cream	krem do rąk	krehm do ronk
lipstick	kredkę do warg	krehtkeh do vahrk
lipstick brush	pędzelek go warg	pehndzehlehk do vahrk
make-up remover pads	płatki do zmywania makijażu	pwahtkee do zmivahñah mahkeeyahzhoo
nail brush	szczotkę do paznokci	shchotkeh do pahznoktshee
nail clippers	cążki do paznokci	tsonshkee do pahznoktshee
nail file	pilnik do paznokci	peelñeek do pahznoktshee
nail lacquer	lakier do paznokci	lahkehr do pahznoktshee
nail scissors	nożyczki do paznokci	nozhichkee do pahznoktshee
perfume	perfumy	pehrfoomi
powder	puder	poodehr
powder puff	puszek	pooshehk
razor	maszynkę	mahshinkeh
razor blades	żyletki	zhilehtkee
rouge	róż	roosh

safety pins	agrafki	ahgrahfkee
shampoo	szampon	shahmpon
shaving brush	pędzel do golenia	pehndzehl do golehñah
shaving cream	krem do golenia	krehm do golehñah
shaving soap	mydło do golenia	midwo do golehñah
soap	mydło	midwo
sun-tan cream	krem do opalania	krehm do opahlahñah
sun-tan oil	olejek do opalania	olehyehk do opahlahñah
talcum powder	talk kosmetyczny	tahlk kosmehtichni
tissues	ligninę	leegñeeneh
toilet paper	papier toaletowy	pahpyehr twahlehtovi
toilet water	wodę kolońską	vodeh koloñskawng
toothbrush	szczoteczkę do zębów	shchotehchkeh do zehmboof
toothpaste	pastę do zębów	pahsteh do zehmboof
towel	ręcznik	rehnchñeek
wash-off face cleanser	płyn do twarzy	pwin do tfahzhi

For your hair

brush	szczotkę do włosów	shchotkeh do vwosoof
comb	grzebień	gzhehbyeñ
curlers	lokówki	lokoofkee
dye	farbę do włosów	fahrbeh do vwosoof
grips (bobby pins)	klipsy do włosów	kleepsi do vwosoof
lacquer	lakier do włosów	lahkehr do vwosoof
oil	oliwę do włosów	oleeveh do vwosoof
piece	treskę	trehskeh
pins	szpilki do włosów	shpeelkee do vwosoof
rollers	lokówki	lokoofkee

For the baby

bib	śliniak	syleeñahk
cream	krem dla dziecka	krehm dlah dzhehtshkah
food	jedzenie dla dziecka	yehdzehñeh dlah dzhehtskah
nappies (diapers)	pieluszki	pyehlooshkee
nappy pins	agrafki	ahgrahfkee
oil	oliwkę dla dziecka	oleefkeh dlah dzhehtskah
powder	puder dziecinny	poodehr dzhehtsheenni
rubber pants	majtki gumowe	mightkee goomoveh

112

Clothing

If you want to buy something specific, prepare yourself in advance. Look at the list of clothing on page 117. Get some idea of the colour, material and size you want. They're all listed in the next few pages.

SHOPPING GUIDE

General

I'd like...	**Proszę...**	prosheh
I want... for a ten-year-old boy.	**Proszę... dla dziesięcio-letniego chłopca.**	proseh... dlah dzhehsyehñtsholehtñehgo hwoptsah
I want something like this.	**Coś w tym rodzaju.**	tsosy ftim rodzahyoo
I like the one in the window.	**Podoba mi się taki jak na wystawie.**	podobah mee syeh tahkee yahk nah vistahvyeh
How much is that per metre?	**Ile kosztuje metr?**	eeleh koshtooyeh mehtr

1 centimetre = 0.39 in.	1 inch = 2.54 cm.
1 metre = 39.27 in.	1 foot = 30.5 cm.
10 metres = 32.81 ft.	1 yard = 0.91 m.

Colour

I want something in...	**Proszę coś...**	prosheh tsosy
I want a darker shade.	**Proszę o ciemniejszy odcień.**	prosheh o tshehmñayshi ottshehñ
I want something to match this.	**Proszę o coś pasującego do tego.**	prosheh o tsosy pahsooyontsehgo do tehgo
I don't like the colour.	**Nie podoba mi się kolor.**	ñeh podobah mee syeh kolor

beige	**beżowy**	behzhovi
black	**czarny**	chahrni
blue	**niebieski**	ñehbyehskee
brown	**brązowy**	bronzovi
cream	**kremowy**	krehmovi
crimson	**purpurowy**	poorpoorovi
emerald	**szmaragdowy**	shmahrahgdovi
fawn	**jasnobrązowy**	yahsnobronzovi
gold	**złoty**	zwoti
green	**zielony**	zyehloni
grey	**szary**	shahri
mauve	**fioletowy**	fyolehtovi
orange	**pomarańczowy**	pomahrahñchovi
pink	**różowy**	roozhovi
purple	**fioletowy**	fyolehtovi
red	**czerwony**	chehrvoni
scarlet	**purpurowy**	poorpoorovi
silver	**srebrny**	srehbrni
tan	**brązowy**	bronzovi
white	**biały**	byahwi
yellow	**żółty**	zhoowti

w paski
(fpahskee)

w kropki
(fkropkee)

w kratkę
(fkrahteh)

z wzorem
(zvzorehm)

Material

Have you anything in...?	**Czy jest coś z...?**	chi yehst tsosy z
Is that made here?	**Czy to jest polskiej produkcji?**	chi to yehst polskay prodooktsyee
hand-made	**ręczna robota**	rehnchnah robotah
imported	**importowane**	eemportovahneh
I want something thinner.	**Proszę o coś cieńszego.**	prosheh o tsosy tshehñshehgo
Have you any better quality?	**Czy jest coś w lepszym gatunku?**	chi yehst tsosy vlehpshim gahtoonkoo

What's it made of?	Z jakiego materiału to jest?	z-yahkehgo mahtehryahwoo to yehst

It may be made of…

cambric	z batystu	zbahtistoo
camel-hair	moheru	mohehroo
chiffon	szyfonu	shifonoo
corduroy	sztruksu	shtrooksoo
cotton	bawełny	bahvehwni
felt	filcu	feeltsoo
flannel	flaneli	flahnehlee
gabardine	gabardyny	gahbahrdini
lace	koronki	koronkee
leather	skóry	skoori
linen	płótna	pwootnah
nylon	nylonu	nilonoo
pique	piki	peekee
poplin	popeliny	popehleeni
rayon	sztucznego jedwabiu	shtoochnehgo yehdvahbyoo
rubber	materiału podgumo wanego	mahtehryahwoo podgoomovahnehgo
satin	atłasu	ahtwahsoo
serge	serży	sehrzhi
silk	jedwabiu	yehdvahbyoo
suede	zamszu	zahmshoo
taffeta	tafty	tahfti
towelling	frote	froteh
tulle	tiulu	tyoolo
tweed	twedu	twehdoo
velvet	aksamitu	ahksahmeetoo
velveteen	pluszu	plooshoo
wool	wełny	vehwni
worsted	samodziału	sahmodzhahwoo

Size

My size is 38.	Mój rozmiar jest trzydzieści osiem.	mooy rozmyahr yehst chshidzhehsytshee osyehm
Our sizes are different at home. Could you measure me?	U nas jest inna numeracja. Czy może pan/pani mnie zmierzyć?	oo nahs yehst eennah noomehrahtsyah. chi mozheh pahn/pahñee mñeh zmyehzhitsh
I don't know the Polish sizes.	Nie znam polskiej numeracji.	ñeh znahm polskay noomehrahtsyee

This is your size

Ladies

	Dresses/suits					
American	10	12	14	16	18	20
British	32	34	36	38	40	42
Polish	38	40	42	44	46	48

	Stockings						Shoes			
American ⎱	8	8½	9	9½	10	10½	6	7	8	9
British ⎰							4½	5½	6½	7½
Polish	0	1	2	3	4	5	36	38	38½	39

Gentlemen

	Suits/overcoats						Shirts			
American ⎱	36	38	40	42	44	46	15	16	17	18
British ⎰										
Polish	46	48	50	52	54	56	38	41	43	44

	Shoes								
American ⎱	5	6	7	8	8½	9	9½	10	11
British ⎰									
Polish	38	39	41	42	43	43	44	44	45

A good fit?

Can I try it on?	**Czy mogę to przymierzyć?**	chi **mo**geh to pshimy**eh**zhitsh
Where's the fitting room?	**Gdzie jest przymierzalnia?**	gdzheh yehst pshimyehz**hah**lñah
Is there a mirror?	**Czy jest lustro?**	chi yehst **loo**stro
Does it fit?	**Czy pasuje?**	chi pah**soo**yeh

FOR NUMBERS, see page 175

It fits very well.	**Bardzo dobrze leży.**	bahrdzo dobzheh lehzhi
It doesn't fit.	**Nie pasuje.**	ñeh pahsooyeh
It's too...	**Jest za...**	yehst zah
short/long	**krótki/długi**	krootkee/dwoogee
tight/loose	**obcisły/luźny**	optsheeswi/loozyni
How long will it take to alter?	**Ile czasu zajmie poprawka?**	eelen chahsoo zighmyeh porahfkah

Shoes

I'd like a pair of...	**Proszę parę...**	prosheh pahreh
shoes/sandals/boots	**butów/sandałów/ botków**	bootoof/sahndahwoof/ botkoof
These are too...	**Są za...**	sawng zah
narrow/wide	**wąskie/szerokie**	vonskeh/shehrokeh
large/small	**duże/małe**	doozheh/mahweh
Do you have a larger size?	**Czy jest większy numer?**	chi yehst vyehnkshi noomehr
I want a smaller size.	**Proszę o mniejszy numer.**	prosheh o mñayshi noomehr
Do you have the same in...?	**Czy są takie same w kolorze...?**	chi sawng tahkeh sahmeh fkolozheh
brown/beige	**brązowym/ beżowym**	bronzovim/behzhovim
black/white	**czarnym/białym**	chahrnim/byahwim

Shoes worn out? Here's the key to getting them fixed again.

Can you repair these shoes?	**Czy może pan zreperować te buty?**	chi mozheh pahn zrehpehrovahtsh teh booti
I want new soles and heels.	**Proszę o nowe podeszwy i obcasy.**	prosheh o noveh podehshfi ee optsahsi
When will they be ready?	**Kiedy będą gotowe?**	kehdi behndawng gotoveh

SHOPPING GUIDE

Clothes and accessories

I would like a/an/some...	Proszę...	prosheh
bathing cap	czepek kąpielowy	chehpehk kompyehlovi
bathing suit	kostium kąpielowy	kostyoom kompyehlovi
bath robe	szlafrok kąpielowy	shlahfrok kompyehlovi
bikini	kostium bikini	kostyoom beekeeñee
blouse	bluzkę	blooskeh
bow tie	muszkę	mooshkeh
bra	stanik	stahñeek
braces (Br.)	szelki	shehlkee
briefs	kalesony	kahlehsoni
cap	czapkę	chahpkeh
cape	kamizelkę	kahmeezehlkeh
coat	płaszcz	pwahshch
costume	kostium	kostyoom
dinner jacket	smoking	smokeenk
dress	sukienkę	sookehnkeh
dressing gown	szlafrok	shlahfrok
evening dress	suknię wieczorową	sookñeh vyehchorovawng
frock	sukienkę	sookehnkeh
fur coat	futro	footro
girdle	majtki elastyczne	mightkee ehlahstichneh
gloves	rękawiczki	rehnkahveechkee
gym shoes	trampki	trahmpkee
handkerchief	chusteczkę	hoostehchkeh
hat	kapelusz	kahpehloosh
jacket	marynarkę	mahrinahrkeh
jeans	dżinsy	jeensi
jumper (Br.)	sweter	sfehtehr
knickers	ciepłe majtki damskie	tshehpweh mightkee dahmskeh
lingerie	bieliznę	byehleezneh
mackintosh	płaszcz nieprzemakalny	pwahshch ñehpshehmahkahlni
necktie	krawat	krahvaht
negligé	peniuar	pehñooahr
nightdress	koszulę nocną	koshooleh notsnawng
overalls	kombinezon	kombeenehzon
overcoat	płaszcz	pwahshch
panties	majtki damskie	mightkee dahmskeh
pants (trousers)	spodnie	spodñeh

pullover	**pulower**	poolovehr
pyjamas	**piżamę**	peezhahmeh
raincoat	**płaszcz od deszczu**	pwahshch od **dehsh**choo
rubber boots	**buty gumowe**	booti goomoveh
sandals	**sandały**	sahndahwi
scarf	**szalik**	shahleek
shirt	**koszulę**	koshooleh
shoes	**buty**	booti
skirt	**spódnicę**	spoodñeetseh
slip	**halkę**	hahlkeh
slippers	**ranne pantofle**	rahnneh pahntofleh
socks	**skarpetki**	skahr**peht**kee
sports jacket	**marynarkę sportową**	mahrinahrkeh sportovawng
stockings	**pończochy**	poñchohi
suit (man's)	**garnitur**	gahrñeetoor
suit (woman's)	**kostium**	kostyoom
suspender belt	**pasek do podwiązek**	**pah**sehk do pod**vyon**zehk
suspenders	**szelki**	shehlkee
swimsuit	**kostium kąpielowy**	**kos**tyoom kompyehlovi
T-shirt	**koszulkę trykotową**	koshoolkeh trikotovawng
tennis shoes	**tenisówki**	tehñeesoofkee
tie	**krawat**	krahvaht
tights	**rajstopy**	righstopi
top coat	**płaszcz**	pwahshch
trousers	**spodnie**	spodñeh
twin set	**bliźniak**	bleezyñahk
underpants(men)	**kalesony**	kahlehsoni
vest (Am.)	**kamizelkę**	kahmee**zehl**keh
vest (Br.)	**podkoszulkę**	potko**shool**keh
waistcoat	**kamizelkę**	kahmee**zehl**keh

belt	**pasek**	**pah**sehk
buckle	**klamrę**	**klah**mreh
button	**guzik**	**goo**zyeek
collar	**kołnierzyk**	kow**ñeh**zhik
elastic	**gumkę**	**goom**keh
lapel	**klapę**	**klah**peh
pocket	**kieszeń**	**keh**shehñ
sleeve	**rękaw**	**rehn**kahf
zipper	**zamek błyskawiczny**	**zah**mehk bwiskah**veech**ni

Electrical appliances and accessories—Records

Voltage in Poland is 220 AC. Plugs are the common European type. An adaptor may prove useful.

I want a plug for this...	**Proszę wtyczkę do...**	prosheh **ftich**keh do
Have you a battery for this...?	**Czy są baterie do tego...?**	chi sawng bah**teh**ryeh do **teh**go
This is broken. Can you repair it?	**Popsuło się. Czy może pan to naprawić?**	po**soo**oo syeh. chi **mozheh** pahn to nah**prah**veetsh
When will it be ready?	**Kiedy będzie gotowe?**	**kehdi behñdzheh go**toveh
I'd like a/an/some...	**Proszę...**	**prosheh**
adaptor	**rozgałęźnik [przełącznik]**	rozgah**weh**ñzyñeek [psheh**won**chñeek]
amplifier	**wzmacniacz**	**vzmahch**ñahch
battery	**baterię**	bah**teh**ryeh
blender	**mikser**	**meek**sehr
clock	**zegar**	**zeh**gahr
wall clock	**zegar ścienny**	**zeh**gahr **syt**shehnni
food mixer	**mikser**	**meek**sehr
hair dryer	**suszarkę do włosów**	soo**shahr**keh do **vwo**soof
iron	**żelazko**	zheh**lahs**ko
travelling iron	**żelazko podrózne**	zheh**lahs**ko po**droozh**neh
kettle	**czajnik**	**chigh**ñeek
percolator	**młynek do kawy**	**mwi**nehk do **kah**vi
plug	**wtyczkę**	**ftich**keh
radio	**radio**	**rah**dyo
car radio	**radio samochodowe**	**rah**dyo sahmoho**do**veh
portable radio	**radio tranzystorowe**	**rah**dyo trahnzisto**ro**veh
record	**płytę**	**pwi**teh
record player (portable)	**adapter (przenośny)**	ah**dahp**tehr (psheh**nos**yni)
shaver	**maszynkę elektryczną do golenia**	mah**shin**keh ehlehk**trich**nawng do go**leh**ñah
speakers	**głośniki**	gwo**syñee**kee

tape recorder	**magnetofon**	mahgnehtofon
cassette	**kasetowy**	kahsehtovi
portable	**przenośny**	pshehnosyni
television	**telewizor**	tehlehveezor
colour	**kolorowy**	kolorovi
portable	**przenośny**	pshehnosyni
toaster	**toster**	tostehr
transformer	**transformator**	trahnsformahtor

Record bar

Have you any records by…?	**Czy są płyty…?**	chi sawng pwiti
Can I listen to this record?	**Czy mogę przesłuchać tę płytę?**	chi mogeh psheh-swoohahtsh teh pwiteh
I'd like a cassette.	**Proszę kasetę.**	prosheh kahsehteh
I want a new needle.	**Proszę nową igłę.**	prosheh novawng eegweh

L.P.	**płyta długogrająca**	pwitah dwoogograhyontsah
45 rpm	**czwórka**	chfoorkah
mono/stereo	**mono/stereo**	mono/stehreho

classical music	**muzyka klasyczna**	moozikah klahsichnah
folk music	**muzyka ludowa**	moozikah loodovah
jazz	**jazz**	jehs
light music	**muzyka lekka**	moozikah lehkkah
orchestral music	**muzyka orkiestrowa**	moozikah orkehstrovah
pop music	**muzyka młodzieżowa**	moozikah mwodzhehzhovah

Men's hairdressing (barber)

I don't speak much Polish.	Nie mówię po polsku.	ñeh moovyeh po polskoo
I want a haircut, please.	Proszę mnie ostrzyc.	prosheh mñeh ost-shits
I'd like a shave.	Proszę mnie ogolić.	prosheh mñeh ogoleetsh
Don't cut it too short.	Proszę mnie za bardzo nie przystrzyc.	prosheh mñeh zah bahrdzo ñeh pshist-shits
Scissors only, please.	Tylko nożyczkami, proszę.	tilko nozhichkahmee prosheh
A razor cut, please.	Strzyżenie brzytwą, proszę.	st-shizheñeh bzhitfawng prosheh
Don't use the clippers.	Bez nożyczek.	behs nozhichehk
Just a trim, please.	Proszę tylko przystrzyc.	prosheh tilko pshist-shits
That's enough off.	Proszę więcej nie ścinać.	prosheh vyehntsay ñeh sytsheenahtsh
A little more off the...	Proszę trochę więcej ściąć...	prosheh troheh vehntsay sytshoñtsh
back	z tyłu	stiwoo
neck	na karku	nah kahrkoo
sides	na bokach	nah bokahh
top	na górze	nah goozheh
Don't use any oil, please.	Proszę nie moczyć.	prosheh ñeh mochitsh
Would you please trim my...?	Proszę przystrzyc...	prosheh pshist-shits
beard	brodę	brodeh
moustache	wąsy	vonsi
sideboards (sideburns)	bokobrody	bokobrodi
How much do I owe you?	Ile płacę?	eeleh pwahtseh

Ladies' hairdressing

Is there... in the hotel?	**Czy jest w hotelu...?**	chi yehst v hotehloo
a hairdresser	**fryzjer**	frizyehr
a beauty salon	**gabinet kosmetyczny**	gahbeeneht kosmehtichni
Can i make an appointment for...?	**Czy mogłabym umówić się na...?**	chi mogwahbim oomooveetsh syeh nah
I'd like it cut and shaped.	**Proszę obciąć i ułożyć.**	prosheh optshoñts ee oowozhitsh
with a fringe	**z grzywką**	zgzhifkawng
page-boy style	**na pazia**	nah pahzyah
a razor cut	**strzyżenie brzytwą**	st-shizhehñeh bzhitfawng
a re-style	**zmiana fryzury**	zmyahnah frizoori
with ringlets	**z loczkami**	zlochkahmee
with waves	**z falami**	sfahlahmee
in a bun	**z kokiem**	skokehm
I want a...	**Proszę...**	prosheh
bleach	**rozjaśnić**	rozyahsyñeetsh
colour rinse	**płukankę koloryzującą**	pwookahnkeh kolorizooyontsawng
dye	**farbowanie**	fahrbovahñeh
permanent	**trwałą**	trfahawng
shampoo and set	**mycie i ułożenie włosów**	mitsheh ee oowozhehneh vwosoov
touch up	**poprawić**	poprahveetsh
the same colour	**ten sam kolor**	tehn sahm kolor
a darker colour	**ciemniejszy kolor**	tshehmñayshi kolor
a lighter colour	**jaśniejszy kolor**	yahsyñayshi kolor
blond/brunette	**blond/na brunetkę**	blont/nah broonehtkeh
Do you have a colour chart?	**Czy ma pani próbki kolorów?**	chi mah pahñee proopkee koloroof
I don't want any hairspray.	**Bez lakieru proszę.**	behs lahkehroo prosheh
I want a...	**Proszę zrobić...**	prosheh zrobeetsh
manicure/pedicure/face-pack	**manicure/pedicure/maseczkę**	mahñeekyoor/pehdeekyoor/mahsehchkeh
massage	**masaż**	mahsahzh

Jeweller's—Watchmaker's

Can you repair this watch?	**Czy może pan naprawić ten zegarek?**	chi **mozheh** pahn nah**prahveetsh** tehn **zehgahrehk**
The glass is broken.	**Zbiło się szkiełko.**	**zbeewo** syeh **shkehwko**
The spring is broken.	**Pękła sprężyna.**	**pehnkwah** sprehn**zhinah**
The strap is broken.	**Zerwał się pasek.**	**zehrvahw** syeh **pahsehk**
I want this watch cleaned.	**Proszę oczyścić ten zegarek.**	**prosheh** o**chisytsheetsh** tehn **zehgahrehk**
When will it be ready?	**Na kiedy będzie gotowy?**	nah **kehdi behñdzheh gotovi**
Could I see that, please?	**Chciałbym/ chciałabym to zobaczyć.**	**htshahw**bim/ **htshahwahbim** to zobah**chitsh**
I'm just looking round.	**Chcę się tylko rozejrzeć.**	htseh syeh **tilko** rozay**zhehtsh**
I want a small present for...	**Chciałbym/ chciałabym mały prezent za...**	**htshahw**bim/ **htshahwahbim mahwi prehzehnt** zah
I don't want anything too expensive.	**Nie chcę nic bardzo drogiego.**	ñeh htseh ñeets **bahrdzo drogehgo**
I want something...	**Proszę o coś...**	**prosheh** o tsosy
better	**lepszego**	leh**pshehgo**
cheaper	**tańszego**	tahñ**shehgo**
simpler	**prostszego**	prost**shehgo**
Have you anything in gold?	**Czy ma pan/pani coś ze złota?**	chi mah pahn/**pahñee** tsosy zeh **zwotah**
Is this real silver?	**Czy to prawdziwe srebro?**	chi to prah**vdzheeveh srehbro**

If it's made of gold, ask:

How many carats is this?	**Ilu karatowe jest to złoto?**	**eeloo** kahrah**toveh** yehst to **zwoto**

When you go to a jeweller's, you've probably got some idea of what you want beforehand. Find out what the article is made of and then look up its name in Polish in the following lists.

What's it made of?

amber	bursztyn	boorshtin
amethyst	ametyst	ahmehtist
chromium	chrom	hrom
copper	miedź	myehtsh
coral	koral	korahl
crystal	kryształ	krishtahw
diamond	diament	dyahmehnt
ebony	heban	hehbahn
emerald	szmaragd	shmahrahkt
enamel	emalia	ehmahlyah
glass	szkło	shkwo
gold	złoto	zwoto
ivory	kość słoniowa	kosytsh swoñovah
jade	nefryt	nehfrit
onyx	onyks	oniks
pearl	perła	pehrwah
pewter	stop cyny z ołowiem	stop tsini zowovyehm
platinum	platyna	plahtinah
ruby	rubin	roobeen
sapphire	szafir	shahfeer
silver	srebro	shrehbro
silver-plate	plater	plahtehr
stainless steel	stal nierdzewna	stahl ñehrdzehvnah
topaz	topaz	topahs
turquoise	turkus	toorkoos

What is it?

I'd like a/an/some...	Proszę...	prosheh
bangle	bransoletę	brahnsolehteh
beads	korale	korahleh
bracelet	bransoletkę	brahnsolehtkeh
charm bracelet	bransoletkę z breloczkami	brahnsolehtkeh zbrehlochkahmee
brooch	broszkę	broshkeh
chain	łańcuszek	wahñtsooshehk
charm	breloczek	brehlochehk
cigarette case	papierośnicę	pahpyehrosyñeetseh
cigarette lighter	zapalniczkę	zahpahlñeechkeh
clip	klips	kleeps

clock	zegar	zehgahr
alarm clock	budzik	boodzheek
travelling clock	budzik podróżny	boodzheek podroozhni
collar stud	spinkę do kołnierzyka	spheenkeh do kowñezhikah
cross	krzyżyk	kshizhik
cuff-links	spinki	speenkee
cutlery	sztućce	shtootshtseh
earrings	kolczyki	kolchikee
jewel box	szkatułkę na biżuterię	shkahtoowkeh nah beezhootehryeh
manicure set	zestaw do manicuru	zehstahf do mahñeekyooroo
necklace	naszyjnik	nahshiyñeek
pendant	wisiorek	veesyorehk
pin	szpilkę	shpeelkeh
powder compact	puderniczkę	poodehrñeechkeh
propelling (mechanical pencil)	ołówek automatyczny	owoovehk ahwtomahtichni
ring	pierścionek	pyehrsytshonehk
engagement ring	pierścionek zaręczynowy	pyehrsytshonehk zahrehnchinovi
signet ring	sygnet	signeht
wedding ring	obrączkę	obronchkeh
rosary	różaniec	roozhahñehts
silverware	srebro stołowe	srehbro stowoveh
snuff box	tabakierkę	tahbahkehrkeh
strap	pasek	pahsehk
chain strap	łańcuszek	wahñtsooshehk
leather strap	pasek skórzany	pahsehk skoozhahni
watch strap	pasek do zegarka	pahsehk do zehgahrkah
tie clip	spinkę do krawata	speenkeh do krahvahtah
tie pin	szpilkę do krawata	shpeelkeh do krahvahtah
vanity case	saszetkę	sahshehtkeh
watch	zegarek	zehgahrehk
pocket watch	zegarek kieszonkowy	zehgahrehk kehshonkovi
with a second-hand	zegarek z sekundnikiem	zehgahrehk ssehkoondñeekehm
wrist watch	zegarek na rękę	zehgahrehk nah rehnkeh

SHOPPING GUIDE

Kiosk

You'll never go far in Poland without finding a *Ruch* kiosk. These sell an enormous variety of goods, including cigarettes, newspapers and magazines, local bus and tram tickets, stamps, stationary, toilet requisites, books, toys and many other odds and ends.

Usually there are only a small number of Western newspapers on sale in Poland. If you don't manage to get one, you'll probably be able to read one in your hotel lounge or at the *Międzynarodowy Klub Książki i Prasy*—the International Book and Press Club.

Apart from the *Ruch* kiosks, cloakroom attendants always have cigarettes. Don't forget that you can get foreign cigarettes in the *Pewex* shop. Cloakroom attendants often have a variety of foreign cigarettes, too. Polish cigarettes vary in price from the very cheap to the moderately expensive. Most of them don't contain Virginia tobacco, but you may very well develop a taste for them during your stay.

Where's the nearest Ruch kiosk?	Gdzie jest najbliższy kiosk Ruchu?	gdzheh yehst nighbleeshshi kyosk roohoo
Where can I buy an English newspaper?	Gdzie mogę kupić angielską gazetę?	gdzheh mogeh koopeetsh ahngIelskawng gahzehteh
Do you have foreign cigarettes?	Czy są papierosy zagraniczne?	chi sawng pahpyehrosi zahgrahñeechneh
I want a/an/some...	Proszę...	prosheh
bus ticket	bilet autobusowy	beeleht ahwtoboosovi
box of cigars	pudełko cygar	poodehwko tsigahr
cigarette case	papierośnicę	pahpyehrosyñeetseh
cigarette holder	cygarniczkę	tsigahrñeechkeh
flints	kamienie do zapalniczki	kahmyehñeh do zahpahlñeechkee
lighter	zapalniczkę	zahpahlñeechkeh
lighter fluid/gas	benzynę/gaz do zapalniczki	behnzineh/gahz do zahpahlñeechkee
magazine	pismo ilustrowane	peesmo eeloostrovahneh
matches	zapałki	zahpahwkee

newspaper	gazetę	gahzehteh
American/English	amerykańską/	ahmehrikahñskawng/
	angielską	ahngehlskawng
packet of cigarettes	paczkę	pahchkeh pahpyehrosoof
	papierosów	
pipe	fajkę	fighkeh
pipe cleaners	wyciory do fajki	vitshori do fighkee
pipe tobacco	tytoń do fajki	titoñ do fighkee
postcard	pocztówkę	pochtoofkeh
stamps	znaczki	znahchkee
tobacco pouch	woreczek na tytoń	vorehchehk nah titoñ
tram ticket	bilet	beeleht trahmwahyovi
	tramwajowy	
wick	knot	knot
Have you any...?	Czy są...?	chi sawng
American cigarettes	amerykańskie	ahmehrikahñskeh
	papierosy	pahpyehrosi
English cigarettes	angielskie	ahngehlskeh pahpyehrosi
	papierosy	
menthol cigarettes	papierosy	pahpyehrosi mehntoloveh
	mentolowe	
I'd like a carton.	Proszę o karton.	prosheh o kahrton

| filter-tipped | z filtrem | sfeeltrehm |
| without filter | bez filtra | behs feeltrah |

SHOPPING GUIDE

And while we're on the subject of cigarettes, suppose you want to offer somebody one?

Would you like a cigarette?	Może pan/pani zapali?	mozheh pahn/pahñee zahpahlee
Try one of these.	Proszę spróbować	prosheh sproobovahtsh teh.
They're very mild.	te. Są bardzo	sawng bahrdzo wahgodneh
	łagodne.	
They're a bit strong.	Są dość mocne.	sawng dosytsh motsneh

And if somebody offers you one?

Thank you.	Dziękuję.	dzhehnkooyeh
No, thanks.	Nie, dziękuję.	ñeh dzhenkooyeh
I don't smoke.	Nie palę.	ñeh pahleh
I've given it up.	Rzuciłem palenie.	zhootsheewehm pahlehñeh

Laundry—Dry cleaning

If your hotel doesn't have its own laundry/dry cleaning service, ask the porter:

Where's the nearest laundry?	**Gdzie jest najbliższa pralnia?**	gdzheh yehst nighbleeshshah prahlñah

Remember to have change for it.

I want these clothes…	**Proszę to ubranie…**	prosheh to oobrahñeh
cleaned	**wyczyścić**	vichisytsheetsh
pressed	**wyprasować**	viprahsovahtsh
ironed	**wyprasować**	viprahsovahtsh
washed	**wyprać**	viprahtsh
When will it be ready?	**Kiedy będzie gotowe?**	kehdi behñdzheh gotoveh
I need it…	**Potrzebuję to…**	pochshehbooyeh to
today	**na dzisiaj**	nah dzheesyigh
tonight	**na dziś wieczór**	nah dzheesy vyehchoor
tomorrow	**na jutro**	nah yootro
before Friday	**przed piątkiem**	psheht pyontkehm
I want it as soon as possible.	**Potrzebuję to jak najprędzej.**	pochshehbooych to yahk nighprehndzay
Can you… this?	**Czy może pan/ pani to…?**	chi mozheh pahn/**pah**ñee to
mend/patch/stitch	**naprawić/załatać/ zaszyć**	nahprahveetsh/ zahwahtahtsh/**zah**shitsh
Can you sew on this button?	**Czy może pan/ pani przyszyć ten guzik?**	chi mozheh pahn/**pah**ñee pshishitsh tehn **goo**zyeek
Can you get this stain out?	**Czy może pan/ pani wywabić tę plamę?**	chi mozheh pahn/**pah**ñee vivahbeetsh teh **plah**meh
Can this be invisibly mended?	**Czy to się da naprawić bez śladu?**	chi to syeh dah nahprahveetsh behs sylahdoo
This isn't mine.	**To nie moje.**	to ñeh **mo**yeh
There's a hole in this.	**Tu jest dziura.**	too yehst **dzhoo**rah

Photography

It's a good idea to bring sufficient film with you, particularly if you're used to a particular brand of colour film. But if you buy locally you'll find the basic still and home-movie exposures are given in German in the instructions with the roll. Even if you don't understand German, the sketches will help you. Processing isn't included in the price of films.

I'd like a film for this camera.	Proszę film do tego aparatu.	prosheh feelm do tehgo ahpahrahtoo
120 (6×6)	sześć na sześć (6×6)	shehsytsh nah shehsytsh
127 (4×4)	cztery na cztery (4×4)	chtehri nah chtehri
35 mm/135 (24×36)	dwadzieścia cztery na trzydzieści sześć (24×36)	dvahdzhehsytshah chtehri nah chshidzhehsytshee shehsytsh
8 mm	ośmiomili-metrowy	osymyomeeleemehtrovi
super 8	ośmiomili-metrowy super	osymyomeeleemehtrovi soopehr
16 mm	szesnastomili-metrowy	shehsnahstomeelee-mehtrovi
20/36 exposures	dwadzieścia/trzydzieści sześć klatek	dvahdzhehsytshah/chshidzhehsytshee shehsytsh klahtehk
this size	tego rodzaju	tehgo rodzahyoo
this ASA/DIN number	tej czułości ASA/DIN	tay choowosytshee ahsah/deen
black and white	czarno-biały	chahrno byahwi
colour negative	kolorowy negatyw	kolorovi nehgahtif
colour slide (transparency)	slidy	slighdi
artificial light type (indoor)	film do robienia zdjęć przy sztucznym oświetleniu	feelm do robyehñah zdyehntsh pshi shtoochnim osyfyehtlehñoo
daylight type (outdoor)	film do robienia zdjęć w słońcu	feelm do robyehñah zdyehntsh fswoñtsoo
fast/fine-grain	czuły/mało czuły	choowi/mahwo choowi

FOR NUMBERS, see page 175

Processing

How much do you charge for developing?	**Ile kosztuje wywołanie filmu?**	eeleh koshtooyeh vivowahñeh feelmoo
I'd like... prints of this negative.	**Proszę... odbitki z tego negatywu.**	prosheh... odbeetkee stehgo nehgahtivoo
Will you enlarge this, please?	**Proszę to powiększyć.**	prosheh to povyehnkshitsh

Accessories

I want a/an/some...	**Proszę...**	prosheh
cable release	**wężyk do zdjęć**	vehnzhik do zdyehñtsh
exposure meter	**światłomierz**	syfyahtwomyehsh
flash bulbs	**lampę błyskową**	lahmpeh bwiskovawng
flash cubes	**lampę kwadra-towową błyskową**	lahmpeh kfahdrahtovawng bwiskovawng
filter	**filtr**	feeltr
red/yellow	**czerwony/żółty**	chehrvoni/zhoowti
ultra violet	**ultrafioletowy**	ooltrahfyolehtovi
lens	**obiektyw**	obyehktif
lens cap	**przykrywkę na obiektyw**	pshikrifkeh nah obyehktif
lens cleaners	**irchę**	eerheh
tripod	**statyw**	stahtif

Broken

This camera doesn't work. Can you repair it?	**Popsuł mi się aparat. Może pan/ pani go naprawić?**	popsoow mee syeh ahpahraht. mozheh pahn/ pahñee go nahprahveetsh
The film is jammed.	**Film się zaciął.**	feelm syeh zahtshow
There's something wrong with the...	**Nie działa...**	ñeh dzhahwah
automatic lens	**automatyczny obiektyw**	ahwtomahtichni obyehktif
exposure counter	**licznik**	leechñeek
light meter	**światłomierz**	syfyahtwomyehsh
shutter	**migawka**	meegahfkah

Provisions

Here's a list of basic food and drink that you might want on a picnic or for the occasional meal at home.

I'd like a/an/some…, please.	Proszę…	prosheh
apples	jabłka	yahpkah
bananas	banany	bahnahni
biscuits (Br.)	herbatniki	hehrbahtñeekee
bread	chleb	hlehp
butter	masło	mahswo
cakes (Br.)	ciastka	tshahstkah
cheese	ser	sehr
chocolate	czekoladę	chehkolahdeh
coffee	kawę	kahveh
cold meat	mięso na zimno	myehnso nah zymno
cookies	herbatniki	hehrbahtñeekee
cooking fat	tłuszcz	twooshch
crackers	suchary	soohahri
crisps	frytki	fritkee
cucumbers	ogórki	ogoorkee
frankfurters	parówki	pahroofkee
ham	szynkę	shinkeh
ice-cream	lody	lodi
lemons	cytryny	tsitrini
lettuce	sałatę	sahwahteh
milk	mleko	mlehko
mustard	musztardę	mooshtahrdeh
oranges	pomarańcze	pomahrahñcheh
pâté	pasztet	pahshteht
pepper	pieprz	pyehpsh
pickles	marynaty	mahrinahti
pork	wieprzowinę	vyehphshoveeneh
potato chips	frytki	fritkee
potatoes	ziemniaki	zyehmñahkee
rolls	bułeczki	boowehchkee
salad	sałatkę	sahwahtkeh
salami	salami	sahlamee
sandwiches	kanapki	kahnahpkee
sausages	kiełbasę	kehwbahseh
spaghetti	spagetti	spahgehttee
sugar	cukier	tsookehr
sweets	cukierki	tsookehrkee
tea	herbatę	hehrbahteh
tomatoes	pomidory	pomeedori

And don't forget...

a bottle opener	**otwieracz do butelek**	otfyehrahch do bootehlehk
a corkscrew	**korkociąg**	korkotshonk
matches	**zapałki**	zahpahwkee
(paper) napkins	**serwetki (papierowe)**	sehrvehtkee (pahpyehroveh)
a can opener	**klucz do konserw**	klooch do konsehrf

Weights and measures

1 kilogram or kilo (kg) = 1000 grams (g)

100 g = 3.5 oz.	½ kg = 1.1 lb.
200 g = 7.0 oz.	1 kg = 2.2 lb.

1 oz. = 28.35 g
1 lb. = 453.60 g

1 litre (l) = 0.88 imp. quarts = 1.06 U.S. quarts

1 imp. quart = 1.14 l	1 U.S. quart = 0.95 l
1 imp. gallon = 4.55 l	1 U.S. gallon = 3.8 l

---

barrel	**beczułka**	bechoowkah
box	**pudełko**	poodehwko
can	**puszka**	pooshkah
carton	**karton**	kahrton
crate	**skrzynka**	skshinkah
jar	**słoik**	swoeek
packet	**paczka**	pahchkah
tin	**puszka**	pooshkah
tube	**tubka**	toopkah

Souvenirs

As a tourist you're allowed to export from Poland a reasonable quantity of souvenirs without paying any export duty. However, if you're contemplating any large purchase or buying something that could be classified as an antique, enquire whether you'll have to pay duty on it. You need a special export licence for some antiques.

For souvenir shopping you can't do better than go to one of the many *Cepelia* shops which specialise in folklore goods. The *Desa* shops are worth visiting if you're interested in household ornaments.

Finally, worth recommending are the fascinating modern art galleries that sell a wide variety of items (not by any means always cheap) from paintings to unique models of silver jewellery.

Here are some ideas for souvenir shopping:

amber	**bursztyn**	boorshtin
candlesticks	**lichtarze**	leehtahzheh
costume jewellery	**biżuteria srebrna**	beezhootehryah srehbrnah
cut glass	**kryształy**	krishtahwi
dolls in folk costume	**laleczki z Cepelii**	lahlehchkee stsehpehlyee
mountaineers' axes	**ciupagi**	tshoopahgee
ornamental cut paper collages	**wycinanki ludowe**	vitsheenahnkee loodoveh
paintings	**malowanki**	mahlovahnkee
printed silk screens	**wzorzyste parawaniki**	vzozhisteh pahrah-vahñeekee
silver goods	**srebro**	srehbro
tapestries	**gobeliny**	gobehleeni
wood carvings of religious figures	**świątki**	syfyontkee
wooden boxes	**pudełeczka drewniane**	poodehwehchkah drehvñahneh

Your money: banks—currency

The Polish monetary system is based on the złoty. There are 100 groszy to one złoty, abbreviated to gr. and zł., respectively. The name *złoty* means "a piece of gold", although today there's not much that you can buy for a one-złoty piece (colloquially called *złotówka*—zwo**toof**kah).

A Polish visa is usually issued on condition that the tourist exchanges a certain amount of money for every day of his stay.

Currency can be changed at a bank, at any of the Orbis offices, at major hotels and at Warsaw airport. Don't accept offers to change money from unauthorised persons.

Credit cards and traveller's cheques are accepted at major hotels, airlines, restaurants and some stores, e.g. *Cepelia* souvenir shops and *Pewex* hard-currency shops.

Hours

Banks are open from 8 a.m. to noon, Monday to Friday; also open one Saturday a month. Orbis offices are open from 8 a.m. to 7 p.m., Monday to Friday, until 5 p.m. on Saturdays.

Before going

Where's the nearest bank/currency-exchange office?	Gdzie jest najbliższy bank/biuro wymiany dewiz?	gdzheh yehst nigh**bleesh**shi bahnk/**byooro** vimyahni dehvees
Where can I cash a traveller's cheque (check)?	Gdzie mogę wymienić czek podróżny?	gdzheh mogeh vimyeh**ńeetsh chehk podroozhni

Inside

I want to change some dollars.	Proszę wymienić mi kilka dolarów.	prosheh vimyehñeetsh mee keelkah dolahroof
I'd like to change some pounds.	Chciałbym/ chciałabym wymienić trochę funtów.	htshahwbim/ htshahwahbim vimyehñeetsh troheh foontoof
Here's my passport.	Oto mój paszport.	oto mooy pashport
What's the exchange rate?	Jaki jest kurs?	yahkee yehst koors
Can you cash a personal cheque?	Czy mogę zrealizować czek?	chi mogeh zrehahlee-zovahtsh chehk
Can you wire my bank in London?	Czy może pan/ pani zatele-grafować do mojego banku w Londynie?	chi mozheh pahn/pañee zahtehlehgrahfovahtsh do moyehgo bahnkoo vlondiñeh
I've a letter of credit.	Mam list kredytowy.	mahm leest krehditovi
an introduction from...	referencje od...	refehrehntsyeh ot
a credit card	kartę kredytową	kahrteh krehditovawng
I'm expecting some money from London. Has it arrived yet?	Oczekuję na przekaz pieniężny z Londynu. Czy już nadszedł?	ochehkooyeh nah pshehkahs pyehñehnzhni zlondinoo. chi joosh nahtsheht
Give me... 1000-złoty notes (bills) and some small change, please.	Proszę... bank-noty tysiączło-towe i trochę drobnych.	prosheh... bahnknoti tisyontszwotoveh ee troheh drobnih
Give me... large notes and the rest in small notes.	Proszę... dużych banknotów a resztę w mniejszych banknotach.	prosheh... doozhih bahnknotoof ah rehshteh v mñayshih bahnknotahh
Could you check that again, please?	Czy może pan/ pani to jeszcze raz sprawdzić?	chi mozheh pahn/pañee to yehshcheh rahs sprahvdzheetsh

Currency converter

In a world of fluctuating currencies, we can offer no more than this do-it-yourself chart. You can get information about current exchange rates from banks, travel agents and tourist offices. Why not fill in this chart, too, for handy reference?

Złotys	£	$
50 groszy		
1 złoty		
2 złotys		
3 złotys		
5 złotys		
10 złotys		
15 złotys		
25 złotys		
50 złotys		
75 złotys		
100 złotys		
250 złotys		
1000 złotys		

FOR NUMBERS, see page 175

At the post office

The post office is indicated by the words *Urząd Pocztowy* or simply *Poczta*. Sometimes you will see the letters PTT (standing for *poczta, telegraf, telefon*). The post office is open from 8 a.m. to 8 p.m. and houses telegraph and telephone as well as mail services. Apart from mailing letters you may wish to buy some of the beautiful stamps that are always on sale in Poland. If you wish to send parcels outside the country, you'll have to take them to one of the special post offices which have a customs office. You can enquire where this is from your local post office.

Mail boxes are painted red, green or blue. Green boxes are for local mail, blue for airmail, and red for all types of mail.

Where's the nearest post office?	**Gdzie jest najbliższa poczta?**	gdzeh yehst nighbleeshshah pochtah
Can you tell me how to get to the post office?	**Jak mogę dostać się do poczty?**	yahk mogeh dostahtsh syeh do pochti
What time does the post office open/close?	**O której (godzinie) otwiera/zamyka się pocztę?**	o ktooray (godzheeñeh) otfyehrah/zahmikah syeh pochteh
What window do I go to for stamps?	**W którym okienku mogę kupić znaczki?**	fktoorim okehnkeo mogeh koopeetsh znahchkee
At which counter can I cash an international money order?	**W którym okienku mogę zrealizować międzynarodowy przekaz pieniężny?**	fktoorim okehnkoo mogeh zrehahleezovahtsh myehndzinahrodovi pshehkahs pyehñehnzhni
I want some stamps, please.	**Proszę trochę znaczków.**	prosheh troheh znahchkoof
What's the postage for a letter/postcard to the USA/to England?	**Ile kosztuje znaczek na list/pocztówkę do USA/Anglii?**	eeleh koshtooyeh znahchehk/pochtoofkeh nah leest do oo ehs ah/ ahnglyee

Do all letters go airmail?	Czy wszystkie listy przesyła się pocztą lotniczą?	chi fshistkeh leesti pshehsiwah syeh pochtawng lotñeechawng
I want to send this parcel.	Chciałbym/ chciałabym nadać tę paczkę.	htshahwbim/ htshahwahbim nahdahtst teh pahchkeh
Do I need to fill in a customs declaration?	Czy muszę wypełnić deklarację celną?	chi moosheh vipehwñeetsh dehklahrahtsyeh tsehlnawng
I want to send this by...	Chcę to nadać...	htseh to nahdahtsh
airmail	pocztą lotniczą	pochtawng lotñeechawng
express (special delivery)	ekspresem	ehksprehsehm
registered mail	jako polecony	yahko polehtsoni
Where is the poste restante (general delivery)?	Gdzie jest poste restante?	gdzheh yehst post rehstahnt
Is there any mail for me? My name is...	Czy są jakieś listy dla mnie? Moje nazwisko...	chi sawng yahkehsy leesti dlah mñeh? moyeh nahzveesko

ZNACZKI	STAMPS
PACZKI	PARCELS
PRZEKAZY	MONEY ORDERS

Cables (telegrams)

Telegraph and telex services are available at large post offices and major hotels.

Where's the (nearest) cable office?	Gdzie jest (najbliższy) urząd telegraficzny?	gdzheh yehst (nighbleeshshi) oozhont tehlehgrahfeechni
I want to send a cable. May I have a form, please?	Chcę nadać telegram. Proszę o druk.	htseh nahdahtsh tehlehgrahm. prosheh o drook
How much is it per word?	Ile się płaci za słowo?	eeleh syeh pwahtshee zah swovo

Telephoning

You can make local and some inter-city calls from public telephones. There are two systems in effect: with older phones you put the money in before you lift the receiver, otherwise you pay when you get the connection. Kiosks and cloakroom attendants often have a phone you can use. Give two or three złotys for a call here.

Request an international line from your hotel or post office. Be prepared for long delays when placing calls outside Europe.

General

Where's the nearest telephone booth?	Gdzie jest najbliższa budka telefoniczna?	gdzheh yehst nigh-bleeshshah bootkah tehlehfoñeechnah
May I use your phone?	Czy mogę skorzystać z telefonu?	chi mogeh skozhistahtsh stehlehfonoo
Have you a telephone directory or...?	Czy ma pan/pani książkę telefoniczną...	chi mah pahn/pahñee ksyonshkeh tehlehfoñeechnawng
Can you help me get this number?	Czy może pan/pani pomóc mi połączyć się z tym numerem?	chi mozheh pahn/pahñee pomoots mee powonchitsh syeh stim noomehrehm

Operator

Do you speak English?	Czy pan/pani mówi po angielsku?	chi pahn/pahñee moovee po ahngehlskoo
Good morning. I want 12 34 56.	Dzień dobry. Proszę 12 34 56.	dzhehñ dobri. prosheh 12 34 56
Can I dial direct?	Czy jest automatyczne połączenie?	chi yehst ahwtomahtichneh powonchehñeh
I want to place a person-to-person call.	Proszę o rozmowę z przywołaniem.	prosheh o rozmoveh s pshivowahñehm

FOR NUMBERS, see page 175

140

| I want to reverse the charges. | **Proszę o rozmowę R.** | prosheh o rozmoveh ehr |
| Will you tell me the cost of the call afterwards? | **Proszę podać mi potem koszt rozmowy.** | prosheh podahtsh mee potehm kosht rozmovi |

Speaking

I want to speak to…	**Proszę…**	prosheh
Would you put me through to…?	**Proszę mnie połączyć z…**	prosheh mñeh powonchitsh z
I want extension…	**Proszę wewnętrzny…**	prosheh vehvnehnchni
Is that…?	**Czy to…?**	chi to
Hallo. This is…	**Halo. Mówi…**	hahlo. moovee

Bad luck

| Would you try again later, please? | **Proszę spróbować później.** | prosheh sproobovahtsh poozyñay |
| Operator, you gave me the wrong number. | **Połączyła mnie pani ze złym numerem.** | powonchiwah mñeh pahñee zeh zwim noomehrehm |

Telephone alphabet

A	**Adam**	ahdahm	M	**Maria**	mahryah
B	**Barbara**	bahrbahrah	N	**Natalia**	nahtahlyah
C	**Celina**	tsehleenah	O	**Olga**	olgah
D	**Dorota**	dorotah	P	**Paweł**	pahvehw
E	**Ewa**	ehvah	R	**Roman**	romahn
F	**Franciszek**	frahntsheeshehk	S	**Stanisław**	stahñeeswahf
G	**Genowefa**	gehnovehfah	T	**Tadeusz**	takdehwoosh
H	**Henryk**	hehnrik	U	**Urszula**	oorshoolah
I	**Irena**	eerehnah	V	**Viktoria**	veektoryah
J	**Jadwiga**	yahdveegah	W	**Wacław**	vahtswahf
K	**Karol**	kahrol	X	**Xantypa**	ksahntipah
L	**Leon**	lehon	Y	**Ypsylon**	ipsilon
Ł	**Łukasz**	wookahsh	Z	**Zygmunt**	zigmoont

Not there

When will she be back?	Kiedy wróci?	kehdi vrootshee
Will you tell her I called? My name's...	Proszę jej powtórzyć że dzwonił/ dzwoniła...	prosheh yay poftoozhitsh zheh dzvoñeew/ dzvoñeewah
Would you ask her to call me?	Proszę poprosić aby do mnie zadzwoniła.	prosheh poprosyeetsh ahbi do mñeh zahdzvoñeewah
Would you take a message, please?	Czy mogę zostawić wiadomość?	chi mogeh zostahveetsh vyahdomosytsh

Charges

| What was the cost of that call? | Ile kosztowała rozmowa? | eeleh koshtovahwah rozmovah |
| I want to pay for the call. | Chcę zapłacić za rozmowę. | htseh zahpwahtsheetsh zah rozmoveh |

Possible answers

Telefon do pana/pani.	There's a telephone call for you.
Proszę pana/panią do telefonu.	You're wanted on the telephone.
Z jakim numerem pan/pani chce rozmawiać?	What number are you calling?
Numer jest zajęty.	The line's engaged.
Nikt nie odpowiada.	There's no answer.
Pomyłka.	You've got the wrong number.
Telefon jest popsuty.	The phone's out of order.
W tej chwili nie ma go.	He's out at the moment.

The car

Filling stations

Drivers of cars hired in Poland can buy petrol (gas) for złotys, but if your vehicle has non-Polish registration plates you must pay with special coupons (available for hard currency at border points, hotels and tourist offices inside and outside Poland). Petrol available is normal (78 octane), super (94 octane) and diesel.

Where's the nearest filling (service) station?	**Gdzie jest najbliższa stacja benzynowa?**	gdzheh yehst nigh-**bleesh**shah **stah**tsyah behnzi**no**vah
I want ten/twenty/fifty litres, please.	**Proszę dziesięć/dwadzieścia/pięćdziesiąt litrów benzyny.**	**pro**sheh **dzheh**syehñtsh/dvah**dzheh**sytshah/pyeh**ñdzheh**syont **lee**troof ben**zi**ni
I want 15 litres of standard/premium.	**Proszę 15 litrów benzyny nisko-oktanowej/wy-sokooktanowej.**	**pro**sheh 15 **lee**troof ben**zi**ni ñeesko-oktah**no**vay/visoko-oktah**no**vay
Give me… złotys worth of petrol (gas).	**Proszę nalać benzyny za … złotych.**	**pro**sheh **nah**lahtsh behn**zi**ni zah… **zwo**tih
Fill the tank, please.	**Proszę napełnić zbiornik.**	**pro**sheh nah**pehw**ñeetsh **zbyor**ñeek
Check the oil and water, please.	**Proszę sprawdzić olej i wodę.**	**pro**sheh **sprahv**dzheetsh **o**lay ee **vo**deh

Fluid measures					
litres	imp. gal.	U.S. gal.	litres	imp. gal.	U.S. gal.
5	1.1	1.3	30	6.6	7.8
10	2.2	2.6	35	7.7	9.1
15	3.3	3.9	40	8.8	10.4
20	4.4	5.2	45	9.9	11.7
25	5.5	6.5	50	11.0	13.0

Give me... litres of oil.	Proszę... litrów oleju.	prosheh... leetroof olayoo
Top up (fill up) the battery with distilled water.	Proszę dopełnić akumulator.	prosheh dopehwñeetsh ahkoomoolahtor
Would you check the tires?	Proszę sprawdzić opony.	prosheh sprahvdzheetsh oponi
The pressure should be one point six front, one point eight rear.	Ciśnienie powinno być jeden i sześć w przednich kołach i jeden i osiem w tylnych.	tsheesyñehñeh poveenno bitsh yehdehn ee shehsytsh fpshehdñeeh kowahh ee yehdehn ee osyehm ftilnih
Can you mend this puncture (fix this flat)?	Proszę naprawić to przebicie.	prosheh nahprahveetsh to pshehbeetsheh
Will you change this tire, please?	Proszę wymienić to koło.	prosheh vimyehñeetsh to kowo

Tire pressure			
lb./sq. in.	kg/cm²	lb./sq. in.	kg/cm²
10	0.7	26	1.8
12	0.8	27	1.9
15	1.1	28	2.0
18	1.3	30	2.1
20	1.4	33	2.3
21	1.5	36	2.5
23	1.6	38	2.7
24	1.7	40	2.8

Would you clean the windscreen (windshield)?	Proszę wyczyścić przednią szybę.	prosheh vichisytsheetsh pshehdñawng shibeh
Have you a road map of this district?	Czy ma pan/pani mapę samochodową tego regionu?	chi mah pahn/pahñee mahpeh sahmohodovawng tehgo rehgyonoo
Where are the toilets?	Gdzie są toalety?	gdzheh sawng twahlehti

Asking the way—Street directions

Excuse me. Can you tell me the way to…?	Przepraszam. Jak dojechać do…?	psheprahshahm yahk doyehhahtsh do
Where does this road lead to?	Dokąd prowadzi ta droga?	dokont provahdzhee tah drogah
Can you show me on this map where I am?	Czy może pan/pani pokazać mi na mapie gdzie teraz jestem?	chi mozheh pahn/pahñee pokahzahtsh mee nah mahpyeh gdzheh tehrahs yehstehm
How far is it to… from here?	Jak daleko jest stąd do…?	yahk dahlehko yehst stond do

Miles into kilometres

1 mile = 1.609 kilometres (km)

miles	10	20	30	40	50	60	70	80	90	100
km	16	32	48	64	80	97	113	129	145	161

Kilometres into miles

1 kilometre (km) = 0.62 miles

km	10	20	30	40	50	60	70	80	90	100	110	120	130
miles	6	12	19	25	31	37	44	50	56	62	68	75	81

Possible answers

Pan/pani jedzie nie tą szosą.	You're on the wrong road.
Proszę jechać prosto.	Go straight ahead.
To jest tam na lewo (prawo).	It's down there on the left (right).
Proszę jechać tędy.	Go that way.
Proszę dojechać do pierwszego (drugiego) skrzyżowania dróg.	Go to the first (second) crossroads.

In the rest of this section we will be more closely concerned with the car itself. We have divided it into two parts:

Part A contains general advice on motoring in Poland. It's essentially for reference, and is therefore to be browsed over, preferably in advance.

Part B is concerned with the practical details of accidents and breakdown. It includes a list of car parts and a list of things that may go wrong with them. All you have to do is to show it to the garage mechanic and get him to point to the items required.

Part A

Customs—Documentation

There are no special formalities for temporarily importing a motor vehicle into Poland. You will require the following documents:

passport and visa;
international insurance certificate (green card), valid for Poland;
international driving licence.

The nationality plate or sticker must be on the car. Seat belts are obligatory.

A red warning triangle—for display on the road in case of accident or breakdown—is obligatory. Crash helmets are compulsory for both riders and passengers on motorcycles and scooters.

Remember that parts of some kinds of Western cars will not be easily available in Poland. It may be a good idea to take a set of spare parts with you. And anyway, with some luck the mechanic will get you on the road again—even if he has to make up a part himself.

Here's my...	To moje...	to moyeh
driving licence	prawo jazdy	prahvo yahzdi
green card	polisa ubez-pieczeniowa	poleesah oobehspyeh-chehñovah
passport	paszport	pahshport
I haven't anything to declare.	Nie mam nic do oclenia.	ñeh mahm ñeets do otslehnah
I've...	Mam...	mahm
250 cigarettes	dwieście pięćdziesiąt sztuk papierosów	dvyehsytsheh pyehñdzhehsyont shtook pahpyehrosoof
a bottle of whisky	butelkę whisky	bootehlkeh wiskee
a bottle of wine	butelkę wina	bootehlkeh veenah
We're staying for...	Będziemy...	behñdzehmi
a week	tydzień	tidzhehñ
two weeks	dwa tygodnie	dvah tigodñeh
a month	miesiąc	myehsyonts

Roads

The classification of roads in Poland is as follows:

| E 22 | international highway |

| T 83 | or | 17 | national highway |

Speed limits: in town, 60 kph (37 mph) except where otherwise indicated; outside town, 90 kph (56 mph).

Surfaces are adequate on arterial routes; secondary roads tend to be rather narrow. Special care should be taken at night when poorly lit carts and pedestrians may be on the roads.

Drive on the right, overtake (pass) on the left. The general rule of give way (yielding) to the right operates in Poland where no road has priority. On roundabouts priority is from the right.

All traffic should give way to trams crossing roundabouts. You mustn't pass a tram if it's at a stop where passengers have to alight on the road. At junctions with traffic lights there are always signs indicating which road has priority. Take notice of these when the lights aren't working. If you aren't used to driving with trams, do take the greatest care, specially when making left-hand turns.

Note: Blood alcohol limit is a strictly enforced zero, and police are entitled to take you for an immediate blood test. They also levy on-the-spot fines for speeding and similar infringements.

Parking

Use your common sense when parking. The police are reasonably lenient with tourists but don't push your luck too far.

Park your vehicle in the direction of the traffic or as indicated on the parking signs. When you park in winter it's best to leave your car in gear but not to put the hand brake on. This'll prevent the rear brake shoes from being frozen in the on position.

Excuse me. May I park here?	**Przepraszam. Czy mogę tutaj zaparkować?**	psheh**prah**sham. chi **mo**geh **too**tigh zahpahr**ko**vahtsh
How long may I park here?	**Ile czasu mogę tutaj parkować?**	**ee**leh **chah**soo **mo**geh **too**tigh pahr**ko**vatsh
What's the charge for parking here?	**Ile się płaci za parkowanie?**	**ee**leh syeh **pwah**tshee zah pahrko**vah**ňeh
Must I leave my lights on?	**Czy muszę zostawić światła postojowe zapalone?**	chi **moo**sheh zos**tah**veetsh **syf**yahtwah posto**yo**veh zahpah**lo**neh

Polish road signs

Here are some of the signs you're likely to encounter in Poland.

DOPUSZCZA SIĘ RUCH LOKALNY	Local traffic only
OBJAZD	Diversion (detour)
PARKING TYLKO DLA SAMOCHODÓW OSOBOWYCH	Parking for private cars
ZAKAZ PARKOWANIA OD GODZ 8–20	No parking from 8 a.m. to 8 p.m.

 beneath a sign indicates that the sign no longer applies; however, the ending of a restriction isn't always marked in this way.

 Learner driver

This sign indicates that the road shown by the thick line is the main road and others have to give way (yield).

The single bar "no waiting" sign usually means that waiting is restricted to only one minute. Read the information on the disc. The double bar "no stopping" sign means that there's to be absolutely no stopping, not even to let passengers alight. Keep an eye open for this no-stopping sign when in the country. The restriction on stopping may apply for a kilometre or more but there'll be only the one sign.

Apart from these few notices, Poland uses the international road signs which are standardized and can be found in use in all Western European countries. You will find the most important of these on pages 160–161.

Part B

Accidents

This section is confined to immediate aid. The legal problems of responsibility and settlement can be taken care of at a later stage.

Your first concern will be for the injured. Note that in Poland only qualified medical personnel may move an injured person.

Is anyone hurt?	Czy jest ktoś ranny?	chi yehst tkosy **rahn**ni
Don't move.	Proszę się nie ruszać.	**prosheh** syeh ñeh **roo**shahtsh
It's all right. Don't worry.	Wszystko w porządku. Proszę się nie przejmować.	**fshist**ko fpozhontkoo. **prosheh** syeh ñeh pshaymovahtsh
Where's the nearest telephone?	Gdzie jest naj-bliższy telefon?	gdzheh yehst nigh-**bleesh**shi tehlehfon
Can I use your telephone? There's been an accident.	Czy mogę skorzystać z tele-fonu? Zdarzył się wypadek.	chi **mogeh** skozhi**stah**tsh sthlehfonoo? **zdah**zhiw syeh vipahdehk
Call a doctor/ambulance, quickly.	Proszę wezwać lekarza/pogo-towie, szybko.	**prosheh vehz**vahtsh lehkahzhah/pogotovyeh **ship**ko
There are people injured.	Są ranni.	sawng **rahñ**ñee

Police—Exchange of information

Please call the police.	Proszę wezwać milicję.	**prosheh vehz**vahtsh meeleets-yeh
There's been an accident.	Zdarzył się wypadek.	**zdah**zhiw syeh vipahdehk
It's about 2 kilo-metres from...	Około 2 kilo-metrów od...	okowo 2 keelomehtroof ot...

CAR—INFORMATION

Here's my name/ address.	**Oto moje nazwisko/adres.**	oto moyeh nahz**vees**ko/ **ah**drehs
Would you mind acting as a witness?	**Czy może pan/ pani podać się za świadka?**	chi mozheh pahn/**pah**ñee podahtsh syeh zah syf**yaht**kah
I'd like an interpreter.	**Proszę o tłumacza.**	prosheh o twoo**mah**chah

Remember to put out a red warning triangle if the car is out of action or impeding traffic.

Breakdown

... and that's what we'll do with this section: break it down into four phases.

1. **On the road**
   You ask where the nearest garage is.

2. **At the garage**
   You tell the mechanic what you think is wrong.

3. **Finding the trouble**
   He tells you what he thinks is wrong.

4. **Getting it fixed**
   You tell him to fix it and, once that lot is over, settle the account (or argue about it).

Phase 1—On the road

Where's the nearest garage?	**Gdzie jest najbliższy warsztat samochodowy?**	gdzheh yehst nigh-**bleesh**shi **vahr**shtaht sahmoho**do**vi
Excuse me. My car has broken down. May I use your phone?	**Przepraszam. Popsuł mi się samochód. Czy mogę zadzwonić?**	psheh**prah**sham. popsoow mee syeh sah**mo**hoot. chi **mo**geh zah**dzvo**ñeetsh

What's the telephone number of the nearest garage?	**Jaki jest numer najbliższego warsztatu samochodowego?**	yahkee yest noomehr nighbleeshshehgo vahr-shtahtoo sahmohodovehgo
I've had a breakdown at...	**Samochód popsuł mi się w...**	sahmohoot popsoow mee syeh v
We're on the road from Cracow to Zakopane, about 30 kilometres from Zakopane.	**Jesteśmy na szosie Kraków–Zakopane około 30 kilometrów od Zakopanego.**	yehstehsymy nah shosyeh krahkoof zahkopahneh okowo 30 keelomehtroof od zahkopahnehgo
Can you send a mechanic?	**Czy może pan/pani przysłać mechanika?**	chi mozheh pahn/pahñee pshiswahtsh mehhahñeekah
Can you send a truck to tow my car?	**Czy może pan/pani przysłać samochód aby przyholować mój samochód?**	chi mozheh pahn/pahñee pshiswahtsh sahmohoot ahbi pshiholovahtsh mooy sahmohoot

Phase 2—At the garage

Can you help me?	**Czy może pan/pani mi pomóc?**	chi mozheh pahn/pahñee mee pomoots
I don't know what's wrong with it.	**Nie wiem co się popsuło.**	ñeh vyehm tso syeh popsoowo
I think there's something wrong with the...	**Sądzę że popsuł/popsuły się...**	sondzeh zheh popsoow/popsoowi syeh
battery	**akumulator**	ahkoomoolahtor
brakes	**hamulce**	hahmooltseh
bulbs	**żarówki**	zhahroofkee
clutch	**sprzęgło**	spshehngwo
cooling system	**układ chłodniczy**	ookwaht hwodñeechi
contact	**połączenie elektro-magnetyczne**	powonchehñeh ehlehktro-magnehtichneh
dynamo	**prądnica**	prondñeetsah
electrical system	**układ elektryczny**	ookwaht ehlektrichni
engine	**silnik**	syeelñeek
gears	**biegi**	byehgee

hand brake	**hamulec ręczny**	hahmoolehts rehnchni
headlight	**światła przednie**	syfyahtwah pshehdñeh
horn	**sygnał**	signahw
ignition system	**układ zapłonowy**	ookwahd zahpwonovi
indicator	**kierunkowskaz**	kehroonkofskahs
lights	**światła**	syfyahtwah
brake light	**światło stopu**	syfyahtwo stopoo
reversing (back up) light	**światło przy jeździe wstecz**	syfyahtwo pshi yehzydzhe fstehch
taillights	**światła tylne**	syfyahtwah tilneh
lubrication system	**układ smarowania**	ookwaht smahrovahñah
pedal	**pedał**	pehdahw
reflectors	**reflektory**	rehflehktori
sparking plugs	**świece**	syfyehtseh
starting motor	**starter**	stahrtehr
steering	**układ kierowniczy**	ookwaht kehrovñeechi
suspension	**amortyzator**	ahmortizahtor
transmission	**przekładnia**	pshehkwahdñah
wheels	**koła**	kowah
wipers	**wycieraczka**	vitshehrahchkah

RIGHT	LEFT	FRONT	BACK
PRAWY	**LEWY**	**PRZEDNI**	**TYLNI**
(prahvi)	(lehvi)	(pshehdñee)	(tilñee)

It's...	Jest...	yehst
bad	**popsuty**	popsooti
blown	**spalony**	spahloni
broken	**popsuty**	popsooti
burnt	**spalony**	spahloni
cracked	**pęknięty**	pehnkñehnti
defective	**wadliwy**	vahdleevi
disconnected	**nie kontaktuje**	ñeh kontahktooyeh
dry	**suchy**	soohi
frozen	**zamarznięty**	zahmahrzñehnti
jammed	**zablokowany**	zahblokovahni
knocking	**bije (stuka)**	beeyeh (stookah)
leaking	**przecieka**	pshehtshehkah
loose	**obluzowany**	obloozovahni
misfiring	**przerywa**	pshehrivah
noisy	**hałaśliwy**	hahwahsyleevi
not working	**nie działa**	ñeh dzhahwah
overheating	**przegrzany**	pshehgzhahni

hort-circuiting	spięcie	spyehñtsheh
lack	obluzowany	obloozovahni
lipping	obłuzowanie (paska)	obloozovahñeh (pahskah)
tuck	zablokowany	zahblokovahni
ibrating	nierówno pracuje	ñehroovno prahtsooyeh
veak	słaby	swahbi
vorn	mocno zużyty	motsno zoozhiti

he car won't start.	Samochód nie chce zapalić.	sahmohoot neh htseh zahpahleetsh
t's locked and the eys are inside.	Samochód jest zamknięty a klucze są w środku.	sahmohoot yehst zahmkñehnti ah kloocheh sawng fsyrotkoo
he fan belt is too lack.	Pasek klinowy jest obluzowany.	pahsehk kleenovi yehst obloozovahni
he radiator is eaking.	Przecieka chłodnica.	pshehtshehkah hwodñeetsah
he idling eeds adjusting.	Należy wyregulować zapłon.	nahlehzhi virehgoolovahtsh zahpwon
he clutch engages. po quickly.•	Sprzęgło ma za mały luz.	spshehngwo mah zah mahwi loos
he steering wheel's ibrating.	Jest za duży luz w kierownicy.	yehst zah doozhi loos fkehrovñeetsi
he wipers are mearing.	Wycieraczki rozmazują brud.	vitshehrahchkee rozmahzooyawng broot
he pneumatic uspension is weak.	Pneumatyczny amortyzator jest słaby.	pnehoomahtichni ahmortizahtor yehst swahbi
he pedal needs djusting.	Trzeba wyregulować pedał.	chshehbah virehgoolovatsh pehdahw

Now that you have explained what's wrong, you'll want to now how long it will take to repair it and arrange yourself ccordingly.

| ow long will it take o find out what's /rong? | Ile czasu potrzeba aby sprawdzić co się popsuło? | eeleh chahsoo pochshehbah ahbi sprahvdzheetsh tso syeh popsoowo |

How long will it take to repair?	**Jak długo będzie trwała reperacja?**	yahk **dwoo**go **beh**ñdzheh **tr**fahwah rehpeh**rah**tsyah
Suppose I come back in half an hour/tomorrow?	**Czy mogę przyjść za pół godziny/ jutro?**	chi **mo**geh pshiysytsh zah poow go**dzhee**ni/**yoo**tro
Can you give me a lift into town?	**Czy może pan/ pani podwieźć mnie do miasta?**	chi **mo**zheh pahn/**pah**ñee pod**vyeh**sytsh mñeh do **myah**stah
Is there a place to stay nearby?	**Gdzie tu można przenocować?**	gdzeh too **mo**zhnah pshehnot**so**vahtsh
May I use your phone?	**Czy mogę skorzystać z telefonu?**	chi **mo**geh sko**zhi**stahtsh stehleh**fo**noo

Phase 3—Finding the trouble

It's up to the mechanic either to find the trouble or to repair it.
All you have to do is hand him the book and point to the text in
Polish below.

**Proszę spojrzeć na tę listę alfabetyczną i pokazać co się popsuło.
Jeśli pański klient chce wiedzieć na czym polega defekt, proszę
wskazać odpowiednie wyrażenie znajdujące się na drugiej liście.***

akumulator	battery
amortyzator	suspension
bieg	gear
baterie akumulatora	battery cells
cewka zapłonowa	ignition coil
chłodnica	radiator
cylinder	cylinder
cylinderek hamulcowy	brake drum
diafragma	diaphragm
filtr	filter
filtr benzyny	petrol filter
filtr oleju	oil filter
filtr powietrza	air filter

* Please look at the following alphabetical list and point to the defective item.
If your customer wants to know what's wrong with it, pick the applicable term
from the next list (broken, short-circuited, etc.).

aźnik	carburettor
łowica silnika	cylinder head
łówne łożyska	main bearings
amulec	brake
abel	cable
able rozdzielacza	distributor leads
able świec	spark plug leads
arter	crankcase
olumna kierownicza	steering column
oła	wheels
orba	crankshaft
ożysko	bearing
kładzina tarczy hamulca	lining
as klinowy wentylatora	fan belt
edał sprzęgła	clutch pedal
ierścienie	rings
ierścienie tłoka	piston rings
latynki	points
łyn akumulatora	battery liquid
ływak	float
neumatyczny amortyzator	pneumatic suspension
ołączenie elektro-magnetyczne	contact
ołączenie mechaniczne	connection
ompa	pump
ompa benzynowa	petrol pump
ompa paliwa	fuel pump
ompa wodna	water pump
ompa wtryskowa	injection pump
rądnica	dynamo (generator)
rzekładnia	transmission
rzekładnia automatyczna	automatic transmission
rzekładnia układu kierowniczego	steering box
rzełącznik świateł	dipswitch
rzerywacz	tappets
esor	shock-absorber
ozdzielacz	distributor
ozrusznik	starter motor
ilnik	engine
krzynia biegów	gear box
mar	grease
prężyny	springs
prężynka zaworu	valve spring
przęgło	clutch
tabilizator	stabilizer

CAR—REPAIRS

świece zapłonowe	spark plugs
szczoteczki	brushes
tarcza sprzęgła	clutch plate
tarcze, szczęki hamulca	shoes
termostat	thermostat
tłok	piston
twornik	starter armature
układ elektryczny	electrical system
układ kierowniczy	steering
wał	shaft
wał korbowy	camshaft
wentylator	fan
układ filtra powietrza	cylinder head gasket
zawór	valve
zębatka i wałek zębaty	rack and pinion
zęby	teeth
złącze	joint
złącze uniwersalne	universal joint

Poniższa lista zawiera wyjaśnienie dotyczące defektu w samochodzie oraz sposobu jego usunięcia.*

bije, stuka	knocking
brudny	dirty
krótki	short
luz	play
naładować	to charge
nie kontaktuje	disconnected
niski	low
obluzować	to loosen
obluzowany	loose
pęknięty	cracked
popsuty	broken
przebicie	puncture
przeciekający	leaking
przegrzany	overheating
przerywa	misfiring
przypiłować	to grind in
rozmontować wszystko	to strip down
słaby	weak
skorodowany	corroded
spalony	burnt
spuścić płyn	to bleed
stukający	vibrating

* The following list contains words about what's wrong as well as what may need to be done with the car.

suchy	dry
szybki	quick
uszczelnić	to tighten
wadliwy	defective
wyczyścić	to clean
wygięty	warped
wymienić	to replace
wymienić wykładziny hamulca	to reline
wyregulować	to adjust
wyrównać	to balance
wysadzony	blown
wysoki	high
za duży luz	to slip
zamarznięty	frozen
zablokowany	jammed, stuck
zmienić	to change
zużyty	worn
zwarcie	short-circuit

Phase 4—Getting it fixed

| Have you found the trouble? | Czy wykrył pan defekt? | chi vikriw pahn dehfehkt |

Now that you know what's wrong, or at least have some idea, you'll want to find out...

Is that serious?	Czy to coś poważnego?	chi to tsosy powahzhnehgo
Can you fix it?	Czy może pan to naprawić?	chi mozheh pahn to nahprahveetsh
Can you do it now?	Czy może pan to zrobić teraz?	chi mozheh pahn to zrobeetsh tehrahs
What's it going to cost?	Ile to będzie kosztowało?	eeleh to behńdzhe koshtovahwo
Have you the necessary spare parts?	Czy ma pan wszystkie potrzebne części zamienne?	chi mah pahn fshistkeh pochshehbneh chehńsytshee zahmyehnneh

What if he says "no"?

Why can't you do it?	**Dlaczego nie może pan tego naprawić?**	dlahcheh go ñeh mozheh pahn tehgo nahprahveetsh
Is it essential to have that part?	**Czy ta część jest absolutnie konieczna?**	chi tah chehñsytsh yest ahpsolootñeh koñehchnah
How long is it going to take to get the spare parts?	**Ile czasu zajmie sprowadzenie części zamiennych?**	eeleh chahsoo zighmyeh sprovahdzeñeh chehñsytshee zahmyehnnih
Where's the nearest garage that can repair it?	**Gdzie jest najbliższy warsztat w którym można to naprawić?**	gdzheh yehst nighbleeshshi vahrshtaht fktoorim mozhnah to nahprahveetsh
Could you get that part made here?	**Czy to może być tutaj zrobione?**	chi to mozheh bitsh tootigh zrobyoneh
Well, can you fix it so that I can get as far as…?	**Czy może pan naprawić to tymczasowo tylko aby można było dojechać do…?**	chi mozheh pahn nahprahveetsh to timchahsovo tilko ahbi mozhnah biwo doyehhahtsh do

If you're really stuck, ask if you can leave the car at the garage.
Contact an automobile association—or hire another car.

Settling the bill

Is everything fixed?	**Czy wszystko jest w porządku?**	chi fshistko yehst fpozhontkoo
How much do I owe you?	**Ile jestem panu winien?**	eeleh yehstehm pahnoo veeñehn

The garage then presents you with a bill. If you're satisfied…

I'll have to change some money.	**Muszę wymienić trochę pieniędzy.**	moosheh vimyehñeetsh troheh pyehññehndzi
Thanks very much for your help.	**Dziękuję za pomoc.**	dzhenkooyeh zah pomots

This is for you.	**To dla pana.**	to dlah **pah**nah

But you may feel that the workmanship is sloppy or that you're paying for work not done. Get the bill itemized. If necessary, get it translated before you pay.

I'd like to check the bill first. Will you itemize the work done?	**Chcę sprawdzić rachunek. Czy może pan wyszczególnić wszystkie pozycje?**	htseh **sprahvdzheetsh rahhoo**nehk. chi **mozheh** pahn vishcheh**gool**ñeetsh **fshist**keh pozits-yeh

If the garage still won't back down—and you're sure you're right—get the help of a third party.

Some international road signs

No vehicles

No entry

No overtaking
(passing)

Oncoming traffic
has priority

Maximum
speed limit

No parking

Caution

Intersection

Dangerous bend
(curve)

Road narrows

Intersection
with secondary
road

Two-way traffic

Dangerous hill

Uneven road

Falling rocks

Give way (yield)

Main road,
thoroughfare

End of restriction

One-way traffic

Traffic goes
this way

Roundabout
(rotary)

Bicycles only

Pedestrians
only

Minimum speed
limit

Keep right
(left if symbol
reversed)

Parking

Hospital

Motorway
(expressway)

Motor vehicles
only

Filling station

No through road

Doctor

If you need medical attention, the simplest thing is to ask your hotel receptionist to arrange it for you. But if you have to arrange it yourself, here's what you should know: you may be able to visit the local *przychodnia rejonowa* (pshi**hod**ñah rehyo-**no**vah—medical centre) or ask them to send a doctor to you. This is the state health service, and this only applies if you're from Britain or some other country which has exchanged health agreements with Poland; so take your National Health card along with you.

Alternatively, you can phone the *Spółdzielnia Lekarzy Specjalistów* (Doctors' Cooperative) and arrange an appointment or home visit. There are also private doctors. The *spółdzielnia* will be able to take care of all your needs, whether they are dental, ophthalmic, or just regular traveller's tummy. In an emergency after 10 p.m. summon the emergency doctor who is on call. In most cities he can be reached by dialling 999.

As you will see, this section has been arranged to enable you and the doctor to communicate. From page 165 to 171, you will find your side of the dialogue on the upper half of each page: the doctor's is on the lower half.

The whole section has been divided into three parts: illness, wounds, nervous tension. Page 171 is concerned with prescriptions and fees.

General

I need a doctor—quickly.	**Proszę prędko wezwać lekarza.**	prosheh **prehn**tko **veh**zvahtsh lehkahzhah
Can you get me a doctor?	**Proszę wezwać lekarza.**	prosheh **veh**zvahtsh lehkahzhah
Is there a doctor in the hotel/house?	**Czy jest lekarz w hotelu/domu?**	chi yehst **leh**kahsh fhotehloo/domoo

Please telephone for a doctor immediately.	Proszę natychmiast zadzwonić po lekarza.	prosheh nahtihmyahst zahdzvoñeetsh po lehkahzhah
Where's there a doctor who speaks English?	Gdzie mogę znaleźć lekarza mówiącego po angielsku?	gdzheh mogeh znahlehsytsh lehkahzhah moovyontsehgo po ahngehlskoo
Where's the doctor's office (surgery)?	Gdzie jest gabinet lekarski?	gdzheh yehst gahbeeneht lehkahrskee
What are the office (surgery) hours?	Jakie są godziny przyjęć?	yahkeh sawng godzheeni pshiyehñtsh
Could the doctor come and see me here?	Czy lekarz moze przyjechać i zbadać mnie tutaj?	chi lehkans mozheh pshiyehhahtsh ee zbahdahtsh mñeh tootigh
What time can the doctor come?	O której (godzinie) może przyjechać lekarz?	o ktooray (godzheeñen) mozheh pshiyehhahtsh lehkahsh

DOCTOR

Symptoms

Use this section to tell the doctor what is wrong. Basically, what he'll require to know is:

What? (ache, pain, bruise, etc.)
Where? (arm, stomach, etc.)
How long? (have you had the trouble)

Before you visit the doctor find out the answers to these questions by glancing through the pages that follow. In this way, you'll save time.

Parts of the body

ankle	kostka	kostkah
appendix	wyrostek	virostehk
arm	ramię	rahmyeh
artery	tętnica	tehntñeetsa
back	plecy	plehtsi
bladder	pęcherz	pehnhehsh
blood	krew	krehf
bone	kość	kosytsh

bowels	jelita	yehleetah
breast	pierś	pyehrsy
cheek	policzek	poleechehk
chest	klatka piersiowa	klahtkah pyehrsyovah
collar-bone	obojczyk	oboychik
ear	ucho	ooho
elbow	łokieć	wokehtsh
eye	oko	oko
finger	palec	pahlehts
foot	stopa	stopah
gland	gruczoł	groochow
hand	ręka	rehnkah
head	głowa	gwovah
heart	serce	sehrtseh
heel	pięta	pyehntah
hip	biodro	byodro
intestines	jelita	yehleetah
jaw	szczęka	shchehnkah
kidney	nerka	nehrkah
knee	kolano	kolahno
knee cap	rzepka	zhehpkah
leg	noga	nogah
lip	warga	vahrgah
liver	wątroba	vontrobah
lung	płuco	pwootso
mouth	usta	oostah
muscle	mięsień	myehñsyeñ
neck	szyja	shiyah
nerve	nerw	nehrf
nose	nos	nos
rib	żebro	zhehbro
shoulder	ramię	rahmyeh
skin	skóra	skoorah
spine	kręgosłup	krehngoswoop
stomach	brzuch	bzhooh
tendon	ścięgno	sytshehngno
thigh	udo	oodo
throat	gardło	gahrdwo
thumb	kciuk	ktshook
toe	palec u nogi	pahlehts oo nogee
tongue	język	yehnzik
tonsils	migdałki	meegdahwkee
urine	mocz	moch
vein	żyła	zhiwah
wrist	nadgarstek	nahdgahrstehk

DOCTOR

PATIENT

Part 1—Illness

I'm not feeling well.	**Źle się czuję.**	zyleh syeh **choo**yeh
I'm ill.	**Jestem chory/chora.**	**yehs**tehm hori/horah
I've got a pain here.	**Boli mnie tutaj.**	**boo**lee mñeh **too**tigh
His/her... hurts.	**Boli go/ją...**	**bo**lee go/yawng
I've got a...	**Mam...**	mahm
headache	**ból głowy**	bool **gwo**vi
backache	**ból w plecach**	bool **fpleh**tsahh
fever	**gorączkę**	**goron**chkeh
sore throat	**ból gardła**	bool **gahr**dwah
I'm constipated.	**Mam obstrukcję.**	mahm op**strook**ts-yeh
I've been vomiting.	**Wymiotowałem.**	vimyoto**vah**wehm

DOCTOR

Część 1—Choroba

Co panu/pani dolega?	What's the trouble?
Gdzie pan/panią boli?	Where does it hurt?
Od jak dawna panu/pani dolega?	How long have you had this pain?
Od jak dawna się pan/pani tak źle czuje?	How long have you been feeling like this?
Proszę zawinąć rękaw.	Roll up your sleeve.
Proszę się rozebrać (do pasa).	Please undress (down to the waist).
Proszę zdjąć spodnie.	Please remove your trousers.

DOCTOR

PATIENT

I feel faint/I feel dizzy.	Czuję się słabo/Mam zawroty głowy.	chooyeh syeh swahbo/mahm zahvroti gwovi
I'm nauseous/shivery.	Mam mdłości/Mam dreszcze.	mahm mdwosytshee/mahm drehshcheh
I/He/She has (a/an)…	Mam…	mahm
abscess	wrzód	vzhoot
asthma	astmę	ahstmeh
boil	czyrak	chirahk
chill	dreszcze	drehshcheh
cold	przeziębienie	pshehzyehmbyehñeh
constipation	obstrukcję	opstrooktsyeh
convulsions	konwulsje	konvoolsyeh
cramps	skurcz	skoorch
diarrhoea	rozwolnienie	rozvolñehñeh
fever	gorączkę	goronchkeh
haemorrhoids	hemoroidy	hehmoroydi
hay fever	katar sienny	kahtahr syehnni

DOCTOR

Proszę się tutaj położyć.	Please lie down over here.
Proszę otworzyć usta.	Open your mouth.
Proszę głęboko oddychać.	Breathe deeply.
Proszę zakaszleć.	Cough, please.
Zmierzę tempaturę.	I'll take your temperature.
Zmierzę ciśnienie.	I'm going to take your blood pressure.
Czy po raz pierwszy to panu/pani dolega?	Is it the first time you've had this?
Zrobię panu/pani zastrzyk.	I'll give you an injection.
Potrzebuję próbkę moczu/stolca.	I want a specimen of your urine/stools.

PATIENT

hernia	**przepuklina**	pshehpook**lee**nah
indigestion	**niestrawność**	ñehs**trahv**nosytsh
inflammation of...	**zapalenie...**	zahpah**leh**ñeh
influenza	**grypa**	**gri**pah
stiff neck	**sztywność karku**	**shtiv**nosytsh **kahr**koo
rheumatism	**reumatyzm**	reh**oo**mahtizm
sunburn	**oparzenie słoneczne**	opah**zheh**ñeh swoh**nehch**neh
sunstroke	**porażenie słoneczne**	porah**zheh**ñeh swoh**nehch**neh
tonsillitis	**zapalenie migdałków**	zahpah**leh**ñeh meeg**dahw**koof
ulcer	**wrzód**	vzhoot
whooping cough	**koklusz**	**kok**loosh
It's nothing serious, I hope?	**Mam nadzieję, że to nic poważnego.**	mahm nah**dzheh**yeh zheh to ñeets povah**zhneh**go
I'd like you to prescribe me some medicine.	**Chciałbym by przepisał mi pan lekarstwo.**	h**tshahw**bim bi psheh-**pee**sahw mee pahn leh**kahr**stfo

DOCTOR

To nic poważnego.	It's nothing to worry about.
Trzeba leżeć przez... dni.	You must stay in bed for... days.
Ma pan/pani...	You've got...
przeziębienie/artretyzm/ zapalenie płuc/grypę/ zatrucie	a cold/arthritis/pneumonia/ influenza/food poisoning
Pan/pani za dużo pali/pije.	You're smoking/drinking too much.
To przemęcznie. Trzeba odpocząć.	You're over-tired. You need a rest.
Musi pan/pani pójść do specjalisty.	I want you to see a specialist.
Musi pan/pani pójść do szpitala na badania.	I want you to go to the hospital for a general check-up.
Przepiszę antybiotyki.	I'll prescribe an antibiotic.

PATIENT

I'm a diabetic.	**Mam cukrzycę.**	mahm tsookshitseh
I have a cardiac condition.	**Cierpię na serce.**	tshehrpyeh nah sehrtseh
I've had a heart attack in...	**Miałem/miałam atak serca w...**	myahwehm/myahwahm ahtahk sehrtsah v
I'm allergic to...	**Mam uczulenie na...**	mahm oochoolehñeh nah
This is my usual medicine.	**Zwykle biorę to lekarstwo.**	zvikleh byoreh to lehkahrstfo
I need this medicine.	**Potrzebuję to lekarstwo.**	pochshehbooyeh to lehkahrstfo
I'm expecting a baby.	**Spodziewam się dziecka.**	spodzhehvahm syeh dzhehtskah
Can I travel?	**Czy mogę podróżować?**	chi mogeh podroozhovahtsh

DOCTOR

Jaką dawkę insuliny pan/pani bierze?	What dose of insulin are you taking?
W zastrzyku czy doustnie?	Injection or oral?
Czym pana/panią leczono?	What treatment have you been having?
Jakie lekarstwo pan/pani brał/brała?	What medicine have you been taking?
To był (lekki) atak serca.	You've had a (slight) heart attack.
W Polsce nie stosujemy...	We don't use... in Poland.
Ale to ma bardzo podobne działanie.	This is very similar.
Kiedy spodziewa się pani rozwiązania?	When is the baby due?
Nie moze pani podróżować aż do...	You can't travel until...

PATIENT

Part 2—Wounds

Could you have a look at this…?	Czy moze mi pan/pani coś poradzić na…?	chi mozheh pahn/pahñee tsosy porahdzheetsh nah
blister	ten pęcherz	tehn pehnhehsh
boil	ten czyrak	tehn chirahk
bruise	ten siniak	tehn syeeñahk
burn	to oparzenie	to opahzhehñeh
cut	to skaleczenie	to skahlehchehñeh
graze	to zadraśnięcie	to zahdrahsyñehñtsheh
insect bite	to ukąszenie	to ookonshehñeh
lump	ten guz	tehn goos
rash	tę wysypkę	teh visipkeh
sting	to ukąszenie	to ookonshehñeh
swelling	tę opuchliznę	teh opoohleezneh
wound	tę ranę	teh rahñeh
I can't move my…	Nie mogę ruszać…	ñeh mogeh rooshahtsh…
It hurts.	To mnie boli.	to mñeh bolee

DOCTOR

Część 2—Rany

Jest infekcja.	It's infected.
Nie ma infekcji.	It's not infected.
Musi pan/pani się prześwietlić.	I want you to have an X-ray.
Jest…	It's…
złamany/zwichnięty przemieszczony/rozdarty	broken/sprained dislocated/torn
Mięsień jest naciągnięty.	You've pulled a muscle.
Dam panu/pani środek antyseptyczny. To nic poważnego.	I'll give you an antiseptic. It's not serious.
Musi pan/pani do mnie jeszcze przyjść za…	I want you to come and see me in… days' time.

DOCTOR

PATIENT

Part 3—Nervous tension

I'm in a nervous state.	Jestem wyczerpany nerwowo.	yehstehm vichehrpahni nehrvovo
I want some sleeping pills.	Proszę o tabletki nasenne.	prosheh o tahblehtkee nahsehnneh
I can't eat/I can't sleep.	Nie mogę jeść/ Nie mogę spać.	ñeh mogeh yehsytsh/ ñeh mogeh spahtsh
I'm having nightmares.	Mam przykre sny.	mahm pshikreh sni
Can you prescribe a...?	Czy może pan/ pani przepisać mi...?	chi mozheh pahn/pahñee pshehpeesahtsh mee
sedative	środek uśmierzający	syrodehk oosymyehzhahyontsi
tranquillizer	środek uspokajający	syrodehk oospahkahyahyontsi
anti-depressant	środek antydepresyjny	syrodehk ahntidehprehsiyni

DOCTOR

Część 3—Nerwy

To wyczerpanie nerwowe.	You're suffering from nervous tension.
Potrzebny panu/pani odpoczynek.	You need a rest.
Jakie pigułki pan/pani brał/brała?	What pills have you been taking?
Ile dziennie?	How many a day?
Od jak dawna pan/pani się tak czuje?	How long have you been feeling like this?
Przepiszę pigułki.	I'll prescribe you some pills.
Przepiszę panu/pani środek uśmierzający.	I'll give you a sedative.

PATIENT

Prescriptions and dosage

What kind of medicine is this?	**Co to za lekarstwo?**	tso to zah lehkahrstfo
How many times a day should I take it?	**Ile razy dziennie trzeba je brać?**	eeleh rahzi dzhehññeh chshehbah yeh brahtsh
Must I swallow them whole?	**Czy trzeba je połykać w całości?**	chi chshehbah yeh powikahtsh ftsahwosytshee

Fee

How much do I owe you?	**Ile się należy?**	eeleh syeh nahlehzhi
Do I pay you now or will you send me your bill?	**Czy mam zapłacić od razu czy przyśle mi pan rachunek?**	chi mahm zahpwahtsheetsh od rahzoo chi pshisyleh mee pahn rahhoonehk
Thank you for your help, Doctor.	**Dziękuję za poradę.**	dzhehnkooyeh zah porahdeh

DOCTOR

DOCTOR

Przepisywanie i dozowanie leków

Proszę zażywać to lekarstwo... łyżeczki co... godziny.	Take... teaspoons of this medicine every... hours.
Proszę zażywać pigułki... i popijać je szklanką wody...	Take... pills with a glass of water...
... razy dziennie	... times a day
przed każdym posiłkiem	before each meal
po każdym posiłku	after each meal
rano	in the morning
wieczorem	at night

Honorarium

Płaci pan/pani... złotych.	That's... złotys, please.
Proszę zapłacić od razu.	Please pay me now.
Prześlę panu/pani rachunek.	I'll send you a bill.

FOR NUMBERS, see page 175

Dentist

Can you recommend a good dentist?	**Czy może pan/ pani polecić mi dobrego dentystę?**	chi mozheh pahn/**pah**ñee po**leht**sheetsh mee do**breh**go deh**ñtis**teh
Can I make an appointment to see Doctor…?	**Czy można zamówić wizytę u doktora…?**	chi **mozh**nah zah**moo**veetsh **vee**ziteh oo dok**to**rah…
Can't you possibly make it earlier than that?	**Czy możnaby wcześniej?**	chi **mozh**nahbi **fchehs**yñay
I've a toothache.	**Boli mnie ząb.**	bolee mñeh zomp
I've an abscess.	**Mam ropę pod zębem.**	mahm ropeh pod **zehm**behm
This tooth hurts.	**Boli mnie ten ząb.**	bolee mñeh tehn zomp
at the top	**na górze**	zah **goo**zheh
at the bottom	**na dole**	nah **do**leh
in the front	**z przodu**	**spsho**doo
at the back	**z tyłu**	**sti**woo
Can you fix it temporarily?	**Czy może pan/ pani zaleczyć go tymczasowo?**	chi mozheh pahn/**pah**ñee zah**leh**chitsh go tim**chah**sovo
I don't want it extracted (pulled).	**Proszę go nie wyrywać.**	prosheh go ñeh viri**vahtsh**
I've lost a filling.	**Wypadła mi plomba.**	vi**pahd**wah mee **plom**bah
The gum is very sore/ The gum is bleeding.	**Boli mnie dziąsło/ Krwawi mi dziąsło.**	bolee mñeh **dzhon**swo/ **krfah**vee mee **dzhon**swo

Dentures

I've broken this denture.	**Pękła mi proteza.**	**pehn**kwah mee pro**teh**zah
Can you repair this denture?	**Czy moze pan/ pani zreperować tę protezę?**	chi mozheh pahn/**pah**ñee zrehpeh**ro**vahtsh teh pro**teh**zheh
When will it be ready?	**Na kiedy będzie gotowa?**	nah **keh**di **beh**ñdzheh go**to**vah

Optician

I've broken my glasses.	Stłukłem okulary.	stwookwehm okoolahri
Can you repair them for me?	Proszę je zreperować.	prosheh yeh zrehpehrovahtsh
When will they be ready?	Na kiedy będą gotowe?	nah kehdi behndawng gotoveh
Can you change the lenses?	Proszę zmienić szkła.	prosheh zmyehñeetsh shkwah
I want some contact lenses.	Proszę o szkła kontaktowe.	prosheh o shkwah kontahktoveh
I want tinted lenses.	Proszę o przyćmione szkła.	prosheh o pshitshmyoneh shkwah
I'd like to buy a pair of binoculars.	Proszę o lornetkę.	prosheh o lornehtkeh
How much do I owe you?	Ile się należy?	eeleh syeh nahlehzhi
Do I pay you now or will you send me your bill?	Czy mam zapłacić teraz czy przyśle mi pan/pani rachunek?	chi mahm zahpwahtsheetsh tehrahs chi pshisyleh mee pahn/pahñee rahhoonehk

FOR NUMBERS, see page 175

OPTICIAN

Reference section

Where do you come from?

Africa	**Afryka**	**ah**frikah
Asia	**Azja**	**ahz**-yah
Australia	**Australia**	ahw**strah**lyah
Austria	**Austria**	**ahw**stryah
Belgium	**Belgia**	**behl**gyah
Bulgaria	**Bułgaria**	boow**gah**ryah
Canada	**Kanada**	kah**nah**dah
Czechoslovakia	**Czechosłowacja**	chehhoswo**vahts**-yah
Denmark	**Dania**	**dah**ñyah
East Germany	**N.R.D.**	ehn ehr deh
England	**Anglia**	**ahn**glyah
Europe	**Europa**	ehw**ro**pah
France	**Francja**	**frahnts**-yah
Great Britain	**Wielka Brytania**	**vyehl**kah bri**tah**ñyah
Hungary	**Węgry**	**vehn**gri
India	**Indie**	**een**dyeh
Ireland	**Irlandia**	eer**lahn**dyah
Italy	**Włochy**	**vwo**hi
Japan	**Japonia**	yah**po**ñyah
Netherlands	**Holandia**	ho**lahn**dyah
New Zealand	**Nowa Zelandia**	**no**vah zeh**lahn**dyah
North America	**Ameryka Północna**	ah**meh**rikah poow**nots**nah
Poland	**Polska**	**pol**skah
Romania	**Rumunia**	roo**moo**ñyah
South Africa	**Afryka Południowa**	**ah**frikah poowood**ño**vah
South America	**Ameryka Południowa**	ah**meh**rikah poowood**ño**vah
Soviet Union	**Związek Radziecki**	**zvyon**zehk rah**dzheht**skee
Sweden	**Szwecja**	**shfehts**-yah
Switzerland	**Szwajcaria**	shfight**sah**ryah
United States	**Stany Zjednoczone**	**stah**ni z-yehdno**cho**neh
West Germany	**R.F.N.**	ehr ehf ehn
Yugoslavia	**Jugosławia**	yoogo**swah**vyah

Numbers

0	zero	**zehr**o
1	jeden	**yehd**ehn
2	dwa	dvah
3	trzy	chshi
4	cztery	**cht**ehri
5	pięć	pyehñtsh
6	sześć	shehsytsh
7	siedem	**syeh**dehm
8	osiem	osyehm
9	dziewięć	**dzheh**vyehñtsh
10	dziesięć	**dzheh**syehñtsh
11	jedenaście	yehdehn**nah**sytsheh
12	dwanaście	dvah**nah**sytsheh
13	trzynaście	chshi**nah**sytsheh
14	czternaście	chtehr**nah**sytsheh
15	piętnaście	pyeht**nah**sytsheh
16	szesnaście	shehs**nah**sytsheh
17	siedemnaście	syehdehm**nah**sytsheh
18	osiemnaście	osyehm**nah**sytsheh
19	dziewiętnaście	dzhehvyeht**nah**sytsheh
20	dwadzieścia	dvah**dzheh**sytshah
21	dwadzieścia jeden	dvah**dzheh**sytshah **yeh**dehn
22	dwadzieścia dwa	dvah**dzheh**sytshah dvah
23	dwadzieścia trzy	dvah**dzheh**sytshah chshi
24	dwadzieścia cztery	dvah**dzheh**sytshah **cht**ehri
25	dwadzieścia pięć	dvah**dzheh**sytshah pyehñtsh
26	dwadzieścia sześć	dvah**dzheh**sytshah shehsytsh
27	dwadzieścia siedem	dvah**dzheh**sytshah **syeh**dehm
28	dwadzieścia osiem	dvah**dzheh**sytshah osyehm
29	dwadzieścia dziewięć	dvah**dzheh**sytshah **dzheh**vyehñtsh
30	trzydzieści	chshi**dzheh**sytshee
31	trzydzieści jeden	chshi**dzheh**sytshee **yeh**dehn
32	trzydzieści dwa	chshi**dzheh**sytshee dvah
33	trzydzieści trzy	chshi**dzheh**sytshee chshi
40	czterdzieści	chtehr**dzheh**sytshee
41	czterdzieści jeden	chtehr**dzheh**sytshee **yeh**dehn
42	czterdzieści dwa	chtehr**dzheh**sytshee dvah
43	czterdzieści trzy	chtehr**dzheh**sytshee chshi
50	pięćdziesiąt	pyehñ**dzheh**syont
51	pięćdziesiąt jeden	pyehñ**dzheh**syont **yeh**dehn
52	pięćdziesiąt dwa	pyehñ**dzheh**syont dvah
53	pięćdziesiąt trzy	pyehñ**dzheh**syont chshi
60	sześćdziesiąt	shehsy**dzheh**syont
61	sześćdziesiąt jeden	shehsy**dzheh**syont **yeh**dehn
62	sześćdziesiąt dwa	shehsy**dzheh**syont dvah

63	sześćdziesiąt trzy	shehsydzhehsyont chshi
70	siedemdziesiąt	syehdehmdzhehsyont
71	siedemdziesiąt jeden	syehdehmdzhehsyont yehdehn
72	siedemdziesiąt dwa	syehdehmdzhehsyont dvah
73	siedemdziesiąt trzy	syehdehmdzhehsyont chshi
80	osiemdziesiąt	osyehmdzhehsyont
81	osiemdziesiąt jeden	osyehmdzhehsyont yehdehn
82	osiemdziesiąt dwa	osyehmdzhehsyont dvah
83	osiemdziesiąt trzy	osyehmdzhehsyont chshi
90	dziewięćdziesiąt	dzhehvyehñdzhehsyont
91	dziewięćdziesiąt jeden	dzhehvyehñdzhehsyont yehdehn
92	dziewięćdziesiąt dwa	dzhehvyehñdzhehsyont dvah
93	dziewięćdziesiąt trzy	dzhehvyehñdzhehsyont chshi
100	sto	sto
101	sto jeden	sto yehdehn
102	sto dwa	sto dvah
110	sto dziesięć	sto dzhehsyehñtsh
120	sto dwadzieścia	sto dvahdzhehsytshah
130	sto trzydzieści	sto chshidzhehsytshee
140	sto czterdzieści	sto chtehrdzhehsytshee
150	sto pięćdziesiąt	sto pyehñdzhehsyont
160	sto sześćdziesiąt	sto shehsydzhehsyont
170	sto siedemdziesiąt	sto syehdehmdzhehsyont
180	sto osiemdziesiąt	sto osyehmdzhehsyont
190	sto dziewięćdziesiąt	sto dzhehvyehñdzhehsyont
200	dwieście	dvyehsytsheh
300	trzysta	chshistah
400	czterysta	chtehristah
500	pięćset	pyehñtseht
600	sześćset	shehsytshseht
700	siedemset	syehdehmseht
800	osiemset	osyehmseht
900	dziewięćset	dzhehvyehñtshseht
1000	tysiąc	tisyonts
1100	tysiąc sto	tisyonts sto
1200	tysiąc dwieście	tisyonts dvyehsytsheh
2000	dwa tysiące	dvah tisyontseh
5000	pięć tysięcy	pyehñtsh tisyehntsi
10,000	dziesięć tysięcy	dzhehsyehñtsh tisyehntsi
50,000	pięćdziesiąt tysięcy	pyehñdzhehsyont tisyehntsi
100,000	sto tysięcy	sto tisyehntsi
1,000,000	milion	meelyon
1,000,000,000	miliard	meelyahrt

first	**pierwszy**	pyehrshi
second	**drugi**	droogee
third	**trzeci**	chshehtshee
fourth	**czwarty**	chfarti
fifth	**piąty**	pyonti
sixth	**szósty**	shoosti
seventh	**siódmy**	syoodmi
eighth	**ósmy**	oosmi
ninth	**dziewiąty**	dzhehvyonti
tenth	**dziesiąty**	dzhehsyonti
once	**raz**	rahs
twice	**dwa razy**	dvah rahzi
three times	**trzy razy**	chshi rahzi
a half	**połowa**	powovah
half a…	**pół…**	poow
half of…	**pół…**	poow
half (adj.)	**połowa**	powovah
a quarter	**ćwiartka**	tshfyahrtkah
one third	**jedna trzecia**	yehdnah chshehtshah
a pair of	**para**	pahrah
a dozen	**tuzin**	toozyeen
1981 (year)	**(rok tysiąc dziewięćset) osiemdziesiąt jeden**	(rok tisyonts dzhehvyehñtshseht) osyehmdzhehsyont yehdehn
1992	**(rok tysiąc dziewięćset) dziewięćdziesiąt dwa**	(rok tisyonts dzhehvyehñtshseht) dzhehvyehñdzhehsyont dvah
2003	**dwa tysiące trzy**	dvah tisyontseh chshi

Time

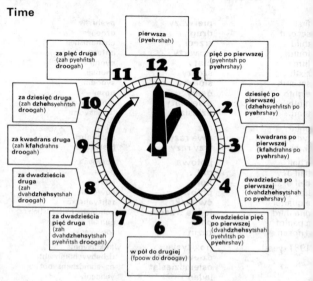

pierwsza
(pyehrshah)

za pięć druga
(zah pyehńtsh **droogah**)

pięć po pierwszej
(pyehntsh po **pyehr**shay)

za dziesięć druga
(zah **dzheh**syehńtsh
droogah)

dziesięć po
pierwszej
(**dzheh**syehńtsh po
pyehrshay)

za kwadrans druga
(zah **kfahd**rahns
droogah)

kwadrans po
pierwszej
(**kfahd**rahns po
pyehrshay)

za dwadzieścia
druga
(zah
dvah**dzheh**sytshah
droogah)

dwadzieścia po
pierwszej
(dvah**dzheh**sytshah
po **pyehr**shay)

za dwadzieścia
pięć druga
(zah
dvah**dzheh**sytshah
pyehńtsh **droogah**)

dwadzieścia pięć
po pierwszej
(dvah**dzheh**sytshah
pyehńtsh po
pyehrshay)

w pół do drugiej
(fpoow do **droogay**)

Useful expressions

What time is it?	**Która godzina?**	ktoorah godzeenah
Excuse me. Can you tell me the time?	**Przepraszam. Która jest godzina?**	pshehprahshahm. ktoorah yehst godzheenah
I'll meet you at... tomorrow.	**Spotkamy się o... jutro.**	spotkahmi syeh o... yootro
I'm sorry I'm late.	**Przepraszam za spóźnienie.**	pshehprahshahm zah spoozyehńeh
after	**po**	po
before	**przed**	psheht
early	**za wcześnie**	zah fchehsyńeh
in time	**punktualnie**	poonktoowahlńeh
late	**spóźniony**	spoozyñoni
midday (noon)	**południe**	powoodñeh
midnight	**północ**	poownots

REFERENCE SECTION

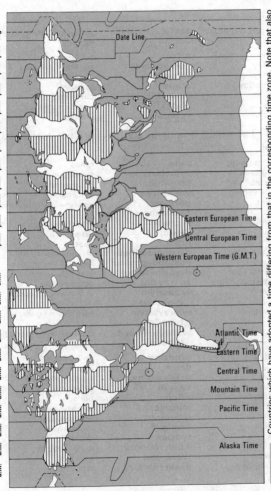

REFERENCE SECTION

1 a.m. 2 a.m. 3 a.m. 4 a.m. 5 a.m. 6 a.m. 7 a.m. 8 a.m. 9 a.m. 10 a.m. 11 a.m. noon 11 a.m. 1 p.m. 2 p.m. 3 p.m. 4 p.m. 5 p.m. 6 p.m. 7 p.m. 8 p.m. 9 p.m. 10 p.m. 11 p.m. mid-night

Date Line

Eastern European Time
Central European Time
Western European Time (G.M.T.)

Atlantic Time
Eastern Time
Central Time
Mountain Time
Pacific Time
Alaska Time

Countries which have adopted a time differing from that in the corresponding time zone. Note that also in the USSR, official time is one hour ahead of the time in each corresponding time zone. In summer, numerous countries advance time one hour ahead of standard time.

Days

What day is it today?	**Jaki jest dzisiaj dzień?**	yahkee yehst **dzhee**syigh dzhehñ
Sunday	**niedziela**	ñeh**dzheh**lah
Monday	**poniedziałek**	poñeh**dzhah**wehk
Tuesday	**wtorek**	**ftorehk**
Wednesday	**środa**	**syrodah**
Thursday	**czwartek**	**chfar**tehk
Friday	**piątek**	**pyon**tehk
Saturday	**sobota**	**sobotah**

Note: The names of months and days are not capitalized in Polish.

REFERENCE SECTION

in the morning	**rano**	**rah**no
during the day	**w ciągu dnia**	**ftshon**goo dñah
in the afternoon	**po południu**	po po**wood**ñoo
in the evening	**wieczorem**	vyeh**cho**rehm
at night	**późnym wieczorem**	**poo**zynim vyeh**cho**rehm
yesterday	**wczoraj**	**fcho**righ
today	**dzisiaj**	**dzhee**syigh
tomorrow	**jutro**	**yoot**ro
the day before	**dzień przedtem**	dzhehñ **psheht**tehm
the next day	**następnego dnia**	nahstehm**pneh**go dñah
two days ago	**dwa dni temu**	dvah dñee **teh**moo
in three days' time	**za trzy dni**	zah chshi dñee
last week	**w zeszłym tygodniu**	**vzeh**shwim tigodñoo
next week	**w przyszłym tygodniu**	**fpshi**shwim tigodñoo
during two weeks	**w ciągu dwóch tygodni**	**ftshon**goo dvooh tigodñee
birthday	**urodziny**	ooro**dzhee**ni
day	**dzień**	dzhehñ
day off	**dzień wolny**	dzhehñ **vol**ni
holiday	**święto**	**syfyeh**nto
holidays	**urlop**	**oor**lop
month	**miesiąc**	**myeh**syonts
name-day	**imieniny**	eemyeh**ñee**ni
vacation	**wakacje**	vah**kah**tsyeh
week	**tydzień**	**ti**dzhehñ
weekday	**dzień roboczy**	dzhehñ robochi
weekend	**week-end**	week-end
working day	**dzień roboczy**	dzhehñ robochi

Months

January	styczeń	stichehñ
February	luty	looti
March	marzec	mahzhehts
April	kwiecień	kfyehtshehñ
May	maj	migh
June	czerwiec	chehrvyehts
July	lipiec	leepyehts
August	sierpień	syehrpyehñ
September	wrzesień	vzhehsyehñ
October	październik	pahzydzhehrñeek
November	listopad	leestopaht
December	grudzień	groodzhehñ

since June	od czerwca	ot chehrftsah
during the month of August	podczas sierpnia	potchahs syehrpñah
last month	w ostatnim miesiącu	vostahtñeem myehsyontsoo
next month	w przyszłym miesiącu	fpshishwim myehsyontsoo
the month before	miesiąc przedtem	myehsyonts pshehttehm
the next month	w przyszłym miesiącu	fpshishwim myehsyontsoo
July 1st	pierwszy stycznia	pyehrshi stichñah
March 17th	siedemnasty marca	syehdehmnahsti mahrtsah

Letter headings are written thus:

Warsaw, August 17, 19. .   **Warszawa, 17 sierpnia, 19. . r**
Cracow, July 1, 19. .   **Kraków, 1 lipca, 19. . r**

Seasons

spring	wiosna	vyosnah
summer	lato	lahto
autumn	jesień	yehsyehñ
winter	zima	zyeemah

in spring	na wiosnę	nah vyosneh
during the summer	w czasie lata	fchahsyeh lahtah
in autumn	na jesieni	nah yehsyehñee
during the winter	w czasie zimy	fchahsyeh zyeemi

Public holidays

These are the main public holidays in Poland when banks, offices and shops are closed.

January 1	New Year's Day
	Easter Monday
May 1	Labour Day
	Corpus Christi
July 22	national holiday commemorating the liberation of Poland in 1944
November 1	All Saints' Day
December 25	Christmas Day
December 26	St. Stephen's Day

The year round...

Here are the average temperatures for some Polish cities (in Fahrenheit degrees).

	Warsaw	Szczecin	Gdańsk	Cracow
January	26.8	30.4	29.3	27.5
February	28.4	31.8	30.4	29.5
March	34.2	37.4	35.1	27.4
April	45.7	45.5	43.3	46.6
May	56.8	55.2	52.3	57.0
June	62.2	61.2	59.5	62.2
July	65.5	64.9	63.7	65.8
August	63.0	62.4	61.9	63.5
September	55.9	56.5	56.3	56.8
October	46.0	47.3	47.1	47.5
November	36.1	38.3	38.1	37.6
December	29.3	32.9	32.4	30.6

REFERENCE SECTION

Conversion tables

Centimetres and inches

To change centimetres into inches, multiply by .39.

To change inches into centimetres, multiply by 2.54.

	in.	feet	yards
1 mm	0,039	0,003	0,001
1 cm	0,39	0,03	0,01
1 dm	3,94	0,32	0,10
1 m	39,40	3,28	1,09

	mm	cm	m
1 in.	25,4	2,54	0,025
1 ft.	304,8	30,48	0,304
1 yd.	914,4	91,44	0,914

(32 metres = 35 yards)

Temperature

To convert Centigrade into degrees Fahrenheit, multiply Centigrade by 1.8 and add 32.

To convert degrees Fahrenheit into Centigrade, subtract 32 from Fahrenheit and divide by 1.8.

Metres and feet

The figure in the middle stands for both metres and feet, e.g.,
1 metre = 3.281 ft. and 1 foot = 0.30 m.

Metres		Feet
0.30	1	3.281
0.61	2	6.563
0.91	3	9.843
1.22	4	13.124
1.52	5	16.403
1.83	6	19.686
2.13	7	22.967
2.44	8	26.248
2.74	9	29.529
3.05	10	32.810
3.35	11	36.091
3.66	12	39.372
3.96	13	42.635
4.27	14	45.934
4.57	15	49.215
4.88	16	52.496
5.18	17	55.777
5.49	18	59.058
5.79	19	62.339
6.10	20	65.620
7.62	25	82.023
15.24	50	164.046
22.86	75	246.069
30.48	100	328.092

REFERENCE SECTION

Other conversion charts

For	see page
Clothing sizes	115
Currency converter	136
Distance (miles-kilometres)	144
Fluid measures	142
Tire pressure	143

Weight conversion

The figure in the middle stands for both kilograms and pounds,
e.g., 1 kilogram = 2.205 lb. and 1 pound = 0.45 kilograms.

Kilograms (kg.)		Avoirdupois pounds
0.45	1	2.205
0.90	2	4.405
1.35	3	6.614
1.80	4	8.818
2.25	5	11.023
2.70	6	13.227
3.15	7	15.432
3.60	8	17.636
4.05	9	19.840
4.50	10	22.045
6.75	15	33.068
9.00	20	44.889
11.25	25	55.113
22.50	50	110.225
33.75	75	165.338
45.00	100	220.450

REFERENCE SECTION

NORTH
POŁNOC
(**poow**nots)

WEST
ZACHÓD
(**zah**hoot)

EAST
WSCHÓD
(fs-hoot)

SOUTH
POŁUDNIE
(po**woo**dñeh)

Common abbreviations

Here are some Polish abbreviations you are likely to encounter.

Al.	Aleja	avenue
CDD	Centralny Dom Dziecka	Central Store for Children
doc.	docent	associate professor
dr	doktor	doctor
dr med.	doktor medycyny	medical doctor
dyr.	dyrektor	director
I. or It.	Informacja	information
inż.	inżynier	engineer
m.	mieszkanie	flat, apartment (in addresses)
mgr	magister	M.A., M.Sc.
MO	Milicja Obywatelska	police
ORMO	Ochotnicza Rezerwa Milicji Obywatelskiej	Reserve Volunteer Police Force
Ob.	Obywatel	citizen (in very official correspondence)
p.	piętro	floor
PKO	Polska Kasa Oszczędności	Polish Savings Bank
PKP	Polskie Koleje Państwowe	Polish State Railways
PKS	Polska Komunikacja Samochodowa	Polish Motor Communication
prof.	profesor	professor
PTTK	Polskie Towarzystwo Turystyczno-Krajoznawcze	Polish Tourist and Country-Lovers Society
PZM or PZMot	Polski Związek Motorowy	Polish Automobile and Motorcycle Federation
PZPR	Polska Zjednoczona Partia Robotnicza	Polish United Workers Party
ul.	ulica	street, road
v-dyr.	wicedyrektor	associate director
W.P.	Wielmożny Pan/Pani	Mr./Mrs. (only in addresses)

What does that sign mean?

You are sure to encounter some of these signs or notices on your trip.

Bilety wyprzedane	Sold out
Ciągnąć	Pull
Ciepła	Hot
Dla pań	Ladies
Dla panów	Gentlemen
Do wynajęcia	To let, for hire
Informacja	Information
Kasa	Cashier's
Kąpiel wzbroniona	No bathing
Nie dotykać	Do not touch
Nie palić	No smoking
Palenie wzbronione	No smoking
Pchać	Push
Proszę zamykać drzwi	Please close the door
Uwaga	Caution
Uwaga, niebezpieczeństwo	Danger
Uwaga zły pies	Beware of the dog
Wejście	Entrance
Winda	Lift (elevator)
Wolny	Vacant
Wstęp wolny	Free entrance
Wstęp wzbroniony	No entrance
Wyjście	Exit
Wyjście zapasowe	Emergency exit
Wyprzedaz	Sales
.... wzbroniona	... forbidden
Zajęty	Occupied
Zamknięty	Closed
Zarezerwowany	Reserved
Zimna	Cold

Emergency

By the time the emergency is upon you it's too late to turn to this page to find the Polish for "I'll scream if you...". So have a look at this short list beforehand—and, if you want to be on the safe side, learn the expressions shown in capitals.

Be quick	**Proszę szybko**	prosheh **shi**pko
Call the police	**Proszę wezwać milicję**	prosheh **vehz**vahtsh meel**eets**yeh
CAREFUL	**OSTROŻNIE**	ostroz**ñeh**
Come here	**Proszę tu przyjść**	prosheh too psiysytsh
Come in	**Proszę wejść**	prosheh vaysytsh
Danger	**Niebezpieczeń-stwo**	ñehbehspyeh**chehñ**stfo
Fire	**Pożar**	po**zhahr**
Gas	**Gaz**	gahs
Get a doctor	**Proszę wezwać lekarza**	prosheh **vehz**vahtsh leh**kah**zhah
Go away	**Proszę odejść**	prosheh odaysytsh
HELP	**RATUNKU**	rah**toon**koo
I'm lost	**Zabłądziłem/ zabłądziłam**	zahbwoñ**dzee**wehm/ zahbwoñ**dzee**wahm
I'm ill	**Jestem chory/ chora**	**yeh**stehm hori/horah
I've lost my...	**Zgubiłem/ Zgubiłam...**	zgoo**bee**wehm/ zgoo**bee**wahm
Leave me alone	**Proszę mnie zostawić w spokoju**	prosheh mñeh zo**stah**veetsh fspo**ko**yoo
Lie down	**Proszę się położyć**	prosheh syeh po**wo**zhitsh
Listen	**Proszę słuchać**	prosheh **swoo**hahtsh
Look	**Patrz**	pahch
LOOK OUT	**UWAGA**	oo**vah**gah
POLICE	**MILICJA**	mee**leets**-yah
Quick	**Szybko**	**shi**pko
STOP	**STOP**	stop
Stop here	**Proszę się tutaj zatrzymać**	prosheh syeh **too**tigh zah**chshi**mahtsh
Stop that man	**Proszę zatrzymać tego człowieka**	prosheh zah**chshi**mahtsh **teh**go chwo**vyeh**kah
STOP THIEF	**ŁAPAĆ ZŁODZIEJA**	**wah**pahtsh zwo**dzhay**ah
Stop or I'll scream	**Proszę przestać bo będę krzyczeć**	prosheh **pshehs**tahtsh bo **behn**deh **kshi**chehtsh

Emergency numbers

Ambulance _____

Fire _____

Police _____

Fill in these as well:

Embassy _____

Consulate _____

Taxi _____

Airport information _____

Orbis _____

Hotel _____

Restaurant _____

_____

_____

_____

_____

_____

_____

_____

_____

_____

_____

_____

Index

REFERENCE SECTION

Arrival	22
Baggage	24
Ballet	83
Bank	134
Basic expressions	11
Beach	87
Body, parts of the	163
Breakfast	34
Bus	72
Cables	138
Camping	90, 106
Car	142
accidents	149
breakdown	150
parts	151
rental	26
repairs	153
Change	25, 134
Chemist	108
Church services	79
Cinema	80
Colours	112
Concerts	83
Conversion	183
Countries	174
Countryside	90
Customs	23, 145
Dancing	84
Dating	96
Days	180
Dentist	172
Directions	25, 144
Doktor	162
Drinks	57
Dry cleaning	128

Eating out	38
appetizers	45
bill	56
complaints	56
dessert	54
drinks	57
eating habits	40
egg dishes	46
fish and seafood	48
fruit	53
game, fowl	51
meat	49
ordering	42
salad	47
seasonings	52
snacks	64
soups	47
vegetables	52
Emergency	188
Equipment	106
Filling stations	142
Friends	93
Games	85
Grammar	17
Hairdressing	121
Hitchhiking	74
Hotel	28
breakfast	34
checking in	29
checking out	37
difficulties	35
registration	32
reservation	25
service	33
Introductions	93

Invitations	95	Shopping guide	97
		bookshop	104
Laundry	128	chemist	108
		clothing	112
Materials	110	electrical appliances	119
Meals	38	general expressions	100
Measurements		hairdresser	121
fluids	132, 142	jeweller	123
km/miles	144	kiosk	126
metric	112, 184	pharmacy	108
sizes (clothing)	115	photography	129
temperature	183	provisions	131
tire pressure	143	records	119
weights	132, 185	shoes	116
Medical section	162	shops, list of	98
Money	25, 134	souvenirs	133
Months	181	toiletry	108
Movies	80	tobacconist	126
		watchmaker	123
Nationalities	174	Sightseeing	75
Night clubs	83	Signs and notices	187
Numbers	175	Sizes (clothing)	115
		Snacks	64
Opera	83	Sports	86
Optician	173	winter sports	89
Parking	147	Taxis	27
Passport control	22	Telegrams	138
Porters	24	Telephone	139
Post office	137	Theatre	80
Pronunciation	7	Time	178
Public holidays	182	Travel	65
		bus	72
		car	142
Records	119	plane	65
Reference section	174	tickets	67
Restaurants	38	train	66
Roads	146	tramway	72
Road signs			
Polish	148	Vodka	60
international	160		
		Weather	94
Seasons	181	Wine	58

REFERENCE SECTION

REFERENCE SECTION

Quick reference page

Please.	**Proszę.**	pro**sheh**
Thank you.	**Dziękuję.**	dzhehn**koo**yeh
Yes/No.	**Tak/nie.**	tahk/ñeh
Excuse me.	**Przepraszam.**	psheh**prah**shahm
Waiter, please.	**Proszę pana/ panią.**	pro**sheh** pah**nah**/ **pah**ñawng
How much is that?	**Ile płacę?**	**ee**leh **pwah**tseh
Where are the toilets?	**Gdzie są toalety?**	gdzheh sawng twah**leh**ti

Toilets	

DLA PANÓW/MĘSKI	**DLA PAŃ/DAMSKI**
(dlah **pah**noof/**mehn**skee)	(dlah pahñ/**dahm**skee)
GENTLEMEN	LADIES

Could you tell me…?	**Czy może mi pan/ pani powiedzieć…?**	chi **mo**zheh mee pahn/ **pah**ñee po**vyeh**dzhehtsh
where/when/why	**gdzie/kiedy/ dlaczego**	gdzheh/**keh**di/dlah**cheh**go
Help me, please.	**Proszę mi pomóc.**	proseh mee po**moots**
What time is it?	**Która godzina?**	**ktoo**rah go**dzhee**nah
Where is the… consulate?	**Gdzie jest konsulat…?**	gdzheh yehst kon**soo**laht
American	**amerykański**	ahmehri**kahñ**skee
British	**brytyjski**	briti**y**skee
Canadian	**kanadyjski**	kahnah**diy**skee
What does this mean? I don't understand.	**Co to znaczy? Nie rozumiem.**	tso to **znah**chi? ñeh ro**zoo**myehm
Do you speak English?	**Czy pan/pani mówi po angielsku?**	chi pahn/**pah**ñee **moo**vee po ahn**gehl**skoo